THE MEDIAEVAL ACADEMY OF AMERICA
PUBLICATION NO. 53

Mediaeval Russian Churches

Kiev in 1854

𝔐ediaeval 𝔕ussian ℭhurches

SAMUEL HAZZARD CROSS

Late Professor of Slavic Languages and Literatures
Harvard University

Edited by

KENNETH JOHN CONANT

Professor of Architecture
Harvard University

THE MEDIAEVAL ACADEMY OF AMERICA
CAMBRIDGE, MASSACHUSETTS
1 9 4 9

The publication of this book was made possible by grants of funds to the Academy from the Carnegie Corporation of New York and the Byzantine Institute, Inc.

PRINTED IN U. S. A. BY THE
CRIMSON PRINTING COMPANY
COLLOTYPE PLATES BY THE MERIDEN GRAVURE COMPANY

Table of Contents

List of Illustrations

(Source, by author's name, in parentheses)

Summary Bibliographical Note

Alpatov, Mikhail V. and Brunov, N. I.—Geschichte der altrussischen Kunst, Augsburg, 1932. A deep study, well illustrated; should be supplemented by other studies on brick and wooden architecture.

Buxton, Daniel Roden—Russian Mediaeval Architecture, Cambridge, England, 1934. A thoroughly good work for general use, richly illustrated.

Grabar', Igor' E. (editor)—Istoriia russkago iskusstva (History of Russian Art), Moscow, 1909; volumes I and II on architecture. A great work, drawn upon in all subsequent studies, including the present essays. Fine and abundant illustrations.

Halle, *Frau* Fannina W.—Die Bauplastik von Wladimir-Ssusdal, Berlin [1929]. Exceptional illustrations.

Krasovskiĭ, Mikhail—Kurs istorii russkoĭ arkhitektury (Course on the History of Russian Architecture), Petrograd, 1916. The published volume is on wooden architecture only.

Lukomskiĭ, Georgiĭ K.—Altrussische Kunst, Munich, 1924.

Lukomskiĭ, Georgiĭ K.—L'Architecture russe du xie au xviie siècle, Paris, 1929. Illustrations of fine quality.

Nekrasov, Alekseĭ I:—Visantiĭskoe i russkoe iskusstvo (Byzantine and Russian Art), Moscow, 1924. A useful handbook.

Nikol'skiĭ, Viktor A.—Istoriia russkago iskusstva (History of Russian Art), Moscow, 1915. Architecture and the other arts up to the eighteenth century.

Réau, Louis—L'Art russe des origines à Pierre le Grand, Paris, 1921. An excellent work of French erudition, but not richly illustrated.

Uspenskiĭ, Aleksandr I.—Ocherkhi po istorii russkago iskusstva (Sketches on Russian Art History), Moscow, 1910. One of a series of publications by a veteran worker in the field.

Voronin, Nikolaĭ N.—Pamiatniki vladimiro-suzdal'skogo zodchestva xi-xiii vekov (Monuments of Vladimir-Suzdal Architecture of the xi-xiii centuries), Moscow, 1945. Geometrical drawings and restorations of interest.

Zabello, S. IA, Ivanov, V., and Maksimov, P.—Russkoe dereviannoe zodchestvo (Russian Wooden Architecture), Moscow, 1942. One of a series of excellent and well illustrated publications by the Academy of Architecture of the U.S.S.R., Office of Theory and History of Architecture.

Preface

The present volume is published by the Mediaeval Academy of America as a tribute to one of the most brilliant and effective men on the roll of its Fellows and officers. Friends and associates will long remember the kindly and positive character of Samuel Hazzard Cross (1891-1946), the quick perception, keen judgment, forthright speech and crackling wit which were his; nor will they forget the unfailing warmth which characterized his intellectual activity and his personal relationships, giving life to both.

As a graduate *summa cum laude* in the Harvard College Class of 1912 he was admirably prepared for the opportunity which a Sheldon Fellowship gave him for study under great teachers in Graz, Berlin, Freiburg, and St. Petersburg before the War of 1914-1918. This experience greatly broadened his field, which had been classics. He undertook studies in German, Russian, comparative literature, and historiography, which became the theme of his scholarly work in later years, and began to teach after taking his Doctor's degree, in 1916.

His career as a teacher was interrupted by military service in World War I, by his diplomatic service with the Commission to Negotiate Peace (in Paris and in Poland), his years as commercial attaché in Brussels and The Hague, and further by three years in business.

He resumed his teaching shortly after his return to this country in 1925. He came back to Harvard in 1928 and in ten years had become a full professor who, in spite of important administrative duties, was doing work of real importance (which included publications) in the Germanic and Slavic fields. He was by that time embarked on his notable career as a valued and active member of various learned societies, and as editor of learned periodicals, including *Speculum*. His influence on students and colleagues alike was very great, especially in the Slavic field; the many projects and studies undertaken with his collaboration or at his suggestion, have shown how fecund this influence was. His untimely death, mourned by devoted friends, left a void which was very difficult to fill.

Dr Cross was always keenly aware of his surroundings, which explains his interest in the mistress art of Architecture. The text which follows is, with trifling editorial changes, the one which he prepared for a series of public lectures sponsored by the Mediaeval Academy of America and delivered at the Fogg Museum, Harvard University, in the fall of 1933. The illustrations are in large measure those which he used at that time, for the difficulty of obtaining Russian photographs has increased rather than diminished in the interval, but certain more recent pictures have been introduced for the sake of clarity and timeliness. The editor, who owes his abiding interest in Russian church architecture to Dr Cross, feels confident that this historical account and artistic analysis will aid many a reader to understand buildings which at first seem very strange. Their study is rewarding from the esthetic point of view, and in a larger sense as well, because their material form resulted from the same tides of influence which produced Russia itself. Thus the churches are guides to the understanding of Russian history, and the present essay on them is a significant part of Dr Cross' message as an interpreter of Slavic culture.

Kenneth John Conant

1. Kiev and Chernigov

From Russian Mediaeval Architecture by D. R. Buxton
Courtesy of Cambridge University Press

1. Kiev and Chernigov

ON THE STAGE of European intellectual progress Russia makes a comparatively late appearance. The early Eastern Slavs who had lived along the middle course of the river Dnieper at least since the time of Herodotus lay in the remote background behind that semibarbaric fusion of Oriental and Greek civilizations which bordered the northern coast of the Black Sea in classical times. These Slavs weathered the invasion and dominiation of the Goths in the second and third centuries of the Christian era, but withdrew into the forests before the successive onslaughts of Huns, Avars, and Bulgars between 375 and 700 A.D. By the eighth century, their territorial extent was more or less fixed, and they were living as rude agriculturalists and hunters, trading in furs and slaves with the Turkish Khazars whose state had grown up in the steppes between the Crimea and the Volga. Numerous small trading posts and strong points established at river junctions and portages already presaged the rise of populous cities, yet so far the various tribes had received no impulse to political combination.

This impulse was supplied from an alien source. Late in the eighth century, adventurous Swedes of Viking type began to push down the northern Russian watercourses in search of a direct contact with Oriental markets. At first their barks traversed the rivers which flow into the Baltic and were thence portaged only to the headwaters of the Volga. Later, at the turn of the next century, these Viking pioneers began to make their way down the Dnieper as well. Settling in the small Slavic towns along the rivers, they soon constituted themselves as a combined garrison and ruling class which rapidly fused with the native stock, but maintained the Scandinavian tradition of discipline, acquisitiveness, and warlike prowess. At the dawn of Russian history about 850, the most energetic clan among these Vikings had made themselves masters of Novgorod, and, appreciating also the strategic importance of Kiev, where a small settlement had existed from prehistoric times, they took possession of this southern point, too, thus gaining control of both ends of the chain of rivers and portages uniting the Baltic with the Black Sea. During the first half of the tenth century, the descendants of Rurik ruling in Kiev and Novgorod concentrated their efforts on subjecting all Slavic tribes within their reach. The tribute in kind (furs, beeswax, honey) gathered from these subject tribes, along with slaves captured on frequent forays, became the material for barter with Oriental traders who brought in the luxury products of the East.

It was not long before the eyes of these Vikings were drawn to the riches of Byzantium. Once in the ninth century (860), an armada of Viking barks from Russia menaced the Greek metropolis, and within the next fifty years commercial exchanges between Kiev and Byzantium became so intense as to require regulation by a lengthy treaty. It is thus about the year 900 that Byzantine cultural influences began to react upon the rudimentary state which the Vikings had set up in conjunction with their Slavic subjects. Some Vikings even took temporary service as mercenaries of the Byzantine emperors, and on their return through Kiev made known to their kinsfolk the splendors of Greek civilization. By 945, a number of these Vikings, who were known to the Greeks as Varangians, were even converted to Christianity, and possessed in Kiev a little chapel dedicated to St Elias, whose fiery chariot facilitated an easy syncretism by which the prophet was identified in their simple minds with their own dynamic Thor, the master of the thunder. In 957, the Princess Olga of Kiev received baptism in Constantinople, and was welcomed with characteristic pomp and ceremony by the Emperor Constantine VII, who has left us a detailed account of the social side of the occasion.

It was Olga's grandson, Vladimir I (Swedish on his father's side and Slavic, i.e., Russian on his mother's, and thus typifying the fusion of Varangian and Russian) who first made Christianity the official religion in the principality of Kiev and thus definitely brought the rising Russian state into direct cultural dependence on Byzantium. From 988, the date of his conversion, close dynastic ties united Kiev with the Greek capital. Though he had to put aside a Scandinavian wife to do so, Vladimir married a sister of the reigning Greek emperors, and became a kinsman of the most exclusive ruling family of his day. Greek priests and schoolmen participated in the organization of the youthful Russian church, and Greek artisans journeyed to Kiev to aid in the erection of churches which Vladimir's ambition soon conceived.

The earliest churches in Kiev, like the Varangian chapel of St Elias and the Church of St Basil which was Vladimir's first venture in ecclesiastical construction, were doubtless humble edifices of wood. Russia possesses, except in the northeast along the Volga, very little stone fit for architectural purposes, and it was not until some local technique was developed in the handling of bricks that masonry became a common structural instrument. Down to modern times, in the more remote districts of northern Russia, wood had been habitually used for the erection of churchly edifices quite as unique in conception and execution as any of the rather more familiar brick structures with stucco facing or whitewashed surface which are the general object of our study in these chapters. Since wood was the prevailing structural material in mediaeval Russia, frequent fires were the rule, and the most primitive wooden churches in Kiev must therefore have disappeared in the recorded conflagrations of the eleventh century, if not even earlier. Almost immediately upon his conversion Vladimir thus devoted himself to the creation of a more permanent architectural monument.

The Church of the Assumption of the Virgin, usually known as the *Desyatinnaya*, the Church of the Tithe (figure 1) because Vladimir donated to its maintenance a tenth of his income, was begun in 989 and consecrated in 996. It suffered severely in the conflagration of 1017, and was plundered by seditious princes in 1171 and 1203, and collapsed under the weight of a crowd of refugees when the Tartars took Kiev in 1240. The church now on the site was built in 1842. The structural and architectural features of the primitive edifice are known chiefly from contemporary descriptions and from excavations conducted intermittently since 1824, but the whole ground plan is as yet not entirely established. The *Desyatinnaya* was designed and constructed by Greek artisans imported for the purpose, and the ground plan of the Kievan structure reflects precisely the features of Byzantine church architecture most prevalent in the tenth century.

You will recall that the close of the Byzantine iconoclastic controversy in 842 had opened a new period of Byzantine architecture which lasted until Constantinople was captured by the Crusaders in 1204. The most characteristic Byzantine church of this period, the *Nea*, in its day a miracle of sumptuous decoration, has unfortunately disappeared, though its lines are reproduced on a smaller scale and consequently with lighter structure in the Palatine Chapel at Palermo, or more exactly in the former church of St Theodosia, now the Gul-jami in Istanbul. The basic ground plan of these churches was a Greek cross inscribed in a rectangle, surmounted by a cupola over the intersection and sometimes with subsidiary smaller cupolas between arms of the cross. At the west was a narthex, or entrance porch, and at the east were three apses, of which the central one contained the altar. In a large church the lateral apses might be chapels with altars of their own. Adjoining the sanctuary at the left, in any case, was a recess (known as the *prothesis*) used for preparation of the communion elements, while a similar recess or apse at the right (*diakonikon*) served as a sacristy or robing room for the celebrants. The sanctuary was set off from the nave by a low railing or balustrade which evolved into the ornate *eikonostasis*, or icon-screen (frequently a high partition faced with gold and jewels and set with numerous icons), containing three doors, of which the central one, known as the royal gate, was reserved for the celebrants. In front of this *eikonostasis*, a raised platform, known as the *soleia*, was intended for lay-readers and cantors; lecterns stood at either side of the *soleia*. Galleries for the women occupied the other three sides of the church. An essential element of Byzantine church architecture of this period, and one which is perhaps more often thought of as essentially Russian, is the handling of the cupolas. The immense dome of St Sophia rests directly on the hemicycles surmounting each side of the central square, with their intervening pendentives. The central intersection of the new-style churches of the inscribed-cross type was relatively much smaller in area than the space under the dome of St Sophia, hence the diameter of the central cupola was proportionately somewhat reduced. The cupola itself, instead of being set directly on lateral hemicycles, was now raised upon a circular or polygonal drum, regularly pierced with windows lighting the nave. The minor cupolas were lower and smaller than the central one, thus providing a pyramidal silhouette. Apart from the fact that the Russian cupola later develops from a hemisphere into the familiar onion shape, these features of Byzantine architecture of this period apply so generally to the earlier mediaeval Russian churches as to merit a moment's attention.

The *Desyatinnaya* corresponds with this basic design. Its plan resembled that of a three-nave basilica, with three semi-circular apses. The few fragments of internal decoration that have been discovered show this church to have been richly adorned with marble columns, a mosaic floor, and both mosaic and frescoes on the walls. The mosaic floor exhibited a pattern of finely drawn separate circles, in green, white, and red colors, without the intertwining features of the Arabic style. Such fragments of the frescoes as have been discovered indicate that its mural decorations were executed with the classic severity of contemporary Byzantine court painting. While it may logically be supposed that the decorations of the cupola, apses, and walls corresponded with the Byzantine convention represented by the *Nea*, there is no direct evidence this was so. Beyond its mere location, its foundations, and the handful of scanty relics picked up on the site, our knowledge of Vladimir's greatest structure is pitifully meager.

Such is not the case, however, with the most conspicuous monument of mediaeval architecture in Kiev, the great Cathedral of St Sophia (figures 2 to 8), which occupied in the eyes of the pre-revolutionary Russian church the same venerable station ascribed by Roman Catholics to the Basilica of St John Lateran or to St Paul outside the Walls. But as you look at the external views of St Sophia, please bear in mind that what at first glance appears most exotic and bizarre, viz., the silhouettes of the cupolas and the wealth of eternal ornament, is not Byzantine or mediaeval Russian at all, but pure Ukrainian baroque, due to restorations undertaken in the early eighteenth century. The antiquities of St Sophia are largely hidden in its interior, and only an exceedingly imperfect idea can now be formed as to its primitive external aspect in the eleventh century. To the eye accustomed to the magnificent proportions, the airy towers, and the flying buttresses of the great Gothic edifices of Western Europe, the first sight of St Sophia, despite its long history, brings a touch of disappointment, since it is first seen from the south side, and exhibits a somewhat foreshortened aspect because its length from east to west is exceeded by its breadth. Its appeal in any case is less to the occidental esthete and amateur than to the antiquary.

There is some disagreement as to the date at which its construction was begun. The great fire known to have taken place in 1017, and certain confused entries in various early annals, have led some scholars to accept this date, instead of 1037, as the year of its beginning. I personally believe in the later date, in view of the tradition that the cathedral was begun by Vladimir's son Yaroslav the Wise, and is the only Kievan structure due to his initiative which still survives. Its completion and decoration required twenty-four years, and it was consecrated in 1061, though Yaroslav and his wife, the Swedish princess Ingigerd, were both entombed within its precincts before it was finished. St Sophia was sacked by the conquering Tartars in 1240. Abandoned from that time until the seventeenth century, its restoration was begun by the metropolitan Peter Mogila in 1632. Reconstruction was resumed under Mazeppa's orders in 1705, and the external aspect of the church remains substantially as he left it. Accurate archaeological study of St Sophia was not undertaken before 1905, and important problems relating to its original design and construction still await solution. The frescoes had been whitewashed over by Peter Mogila and the Uniates in the seventeenth century; the work of uncovering them was begun in 1848, but it was not until thirty years later that the great mosaics of the main cupola were discovered.

The basic ground plan of St Sophia presents a somewhat unusual type of cruciform church with five naves (figures 3, 4). It was constructed of square blocks of red granite (quartzite) fixed in pink cement. In its primitive aspect the church was rather oblong than square. On three sides (south, west, and north), it was surrounded by a one-story arcade about twenty-four feet in width and eighteen feet high. At the west end of the cathedral, at the ends of the arcades, were built two towers, one on the northwest corner, and the other at a distance of some twenty-one feet from the southwest corner (figure 5). Each tower contains a stone staircase leading to the galleries. The present southern tower was erected after the rest of the structure had been completed, and connected up with the primitive structure in the late eleventh or early twelfth century. The modern external silhouette of St Sophia, exotic in itself, completely disguises the primitive outline. As originally constructed, the cathedral had thirteen cupolas, typifying Christ and his apostles. Such symbolism is not unusual, since later, in the north, we find churches with seven cupolas typifying the seven orders of angels. The central cupola was surrounded by four smaller ones, two over the chief lateral altars and two over the tribunes. Outside these four there were eight others, two over the extreme north and south corner altars (figure 6) and three respectively at the north and south corners of the tribunes outside the larger ones which adjoin the central cupola. These thirteen cupolas are quite apart from the stairway towers. In the course of reconstruction, the original lateral arcades were raised to two stories and supplemented by a second set of the same height and nearly twice their width. It is these extensions which give the church its present quadrangular aspect with the longer axis extending north and south. The reconstruction also entailed some modification of the original layout of cupolas. The drums of the central one and the surrounding four seem to have been somewhat elongated and they were provided with striking new roofs. The other eight were topped with simple rounded caps which practically lose them to the modern eye. Cupolas were added to the two towers, and four others were set up over the new parts of the church: two each in the middle of each side elevation over the new two-story wings, and two at right and left of the apses over the second story imposed on the original lateral arcades. This arrangement gives St Sophia in its modern aspect eleven large cupolas exclusive of the eight small ones of the primitive structure which are now overshadowed and scarcely visible. The modern church by actual count thus has nineteen cupolas of various sizes and designs.

Complex as this modern aspect is, the original construction with thirteen cupolas is still more enigmatic, since there is apparently no Byzantine or Oriental parallel. The only valid suggestion is that the idea was derived from earlier wooden churches, since the tradition is preserved that the first wood church of St Sophia at Novgorod, which was burned in 1045, likewise had thirteen 'vierkhi' (just possibly cupolas). Curiously enough, the experiment was never repeated in Novgorod itself, as far as we know, though examples of many-domed churches are by no means rare in later Russian architectural history. In its architectural silhouette, however, St Sophia stands out as an independent Russian artistic creation. At one time the impression was current that the design of St Sophia was traceable to Caucasian influences, but this opinion has appreciably lost ground among recent investigators.

The interior of St Sophia (figure 7) reveals a large number of masonry piers. In the center is a space shaped like a Greek cross, at the corners of which are twelve piers which support the arches under the galleries. Comparatively little marble went into the construction of St Sophia, and such as was used was confined to decorative rather than utilitarian purposes, except in the mosaic floor, where it was combined with dark red granite. In this respect St Sophia was definitely more modest than the *Desyatinnaya*. Each pier is topped by a simple thin slab of red slate to distribute the weight supported. The piers were originally decorated with colored frescoes, some of which have now disappeared. The gallery rails are composed of slabs of fine-grained dark-red granite pierced with ornamental designs.

In spite of some losses through the wear and decay of centuries, the mosaic and fresco decorations in St Sophia still reward long and attentive examination. The mosaics are of particular brilliance and impressiveness. In the main cupola appears Christ as Pantocrator, his right hand raised in blessing, while his left holds a book. He is surrounded by four archangels, each of whom holds a globe in the right hand and a labarum in the left. The pendentives at the corners are occupied by the evangelists, carrying the gospel to the four corners of the world. In the conch of the altar apse appears the majestic mosaic of the Virgin Orante, traditionally known as the 'Unbroken Wall' (*nerushimaya stena*). This mosaic figure is of heroic proportions, some fifteen feet in height, with arms upraised in supplication. She typifies the church on earth and the eternal intercession of the Immaculate Mother. She stands alone against a gold background, clad in a purple *omophorion*, which is thrown over the head and around the shoulders. Beneath it, her chiton falls in graceful folds to the tips of red slippers contrasting with the simplicity of the garment itself. The type of the Virgin is matronly: her face is an elongated oval, with a slender straight nose and an expression severely calm, yet devoid of the dour character sometimes evident in late Byzantine representations. Owing to its position on a curved surface, the mosaic is not accurately represented by ordinary photographs, which show the figure as only eight heads high, though it is actually nearer ten. On the other hand, the pictures show the figure as it meets the eye, without regard to the mechanical elongation carried out by the artist to compensate for the concave surface on which he was working. Below the figure of the Virgin is a mosaic of the Eucharist, and on either side of the arch of the altar apse a mosaic of the Annunciation with the Archangel Gabriel on the left and the Virgin on the right.

The frescoes of St Sophia have suffered extensively from wear and restoration, so that more recent discoveries among them, particularly figures of St Nataliya and St Adrian, were doubly welcome examples of transplanted Byzantine art. Apart from the various complex elements of religious portraiture and symbolism offered by the mural decorations of St Sophia, I should like to call your attention to the striking frescoes on the walls of the staircases leading to the galleries, which represent Byzantine hunting scenes and hippodrome spectacles (figure 8). These latter might seem out of place in a religious edifice, except for the probability that the stairways connected with the prince's palace which has long since disappeared. These frescoes are of peculiar interest as depicting in considerable detail the elaborate spectacles presented at Christmas time in the Hippodrome at Constantinople before the Byzantine emperor and his suite. Unfortunately the staircases are very dark.

I have placed so much emphasis on St Sophia in Kiev because, despite its admittedly trivial modern exterior, it is in basic design and internal decoration the outstanding monument of the period and a veritable treasure house for the study of eleventh century Byzantine decorative art.

In actual antiquity, however, St Sophia is slightly inferior to the considerably less elaborate Cathedral of the Transfiguration at Chernigov, some seventy-five miles northeast of Kiev (figure 9). This church was begun some years before St

Sophia by Prince Mstislav, the brother of the originator of the latter, and it is recorded in the mediaeval Russian annals that at his death in 1036 its walls had been raised to a point higher than a man on horseback could reach with his hand. The church was completed by Mstislav's son. It was destroyed in the Second World War. Chernigov itself was burned by the Tartars in 1237, and the cathedral remained in a dilapidated state until partially restored by private initiative in 1675. It was again damaged by fire in 1750. The final modern restoration was begun in 1790 under Catherine II and completed in 1798 during the reign of her son and successor Paul I. The Cathedral of the Transfiguration at Chernigov was originally a three-naved basilica with three corresponding semicircular apses and five round cupolas, one large one over the central arches and four smaller ones at the corners. The narthex extended the full breadth of the three naves. One tower containing a staircase to the galleries originally adjoined the northwest corner of the façade. Since half this tower had fallen after the fire of 1750, the renovators of Catherine's day added a second balancing tower at the southern angle, topping both with conical spires which now give the church an extraordinarily non-Russian aspect. At the same time, an additional aisle, later replaced by a porch, was added behind each tower. The basic ground plan was quite similar to that of the *Desyatinnaya* in Kiev. The Cathedral of the Transfiguration was not a large church: the height of its main cupola was only ninety feet. A striking feature of its design is a use of marble considerably more extensive than that observed in St Sophia at Kiev. Not only the two columns supporting the altar arch but also the four which support the main cupola are of marble, and the arches under the small cupolas rest on impost blocks of the same material. The primitive gallery, which originally occupied three sides of the church, was preserved only on the west side; it was faced with a balustrade composed of red slate slabs resembling those used in St Sophia for the same purpose. The close analogies in design between the Cathedral of the Transfiguration and the *Desyatinnaya* in Kiev have led naturally to the supposition that the Greek artisans employed for the latter also participated in the construction of the church at Chernigov. Very little of the primitive decoration of the Church of the Transfiguration has been preserved, but among the remnants of antique frescoed figures is one of a picturesque female martyr robed in a stole and believed to represent St Thecla, which may be considered one of the finest examples of early Russian painting.

Another aspect of church architecture in Chernigov is presented by the Church of the Assumption in the Yeletsa Monastery (figure 10). Constructed in the twelfth century, the proportions of this church closely resemble those of the Cathedral of the Assumption in the Crypt Monastery at Kiev, which we shall discuss briefly in a moment. The church originally had but one cupola over the center, the two smaller ones being of modern construction. The church shows some evidences of Western influence in the frieze of the façades, as well as in the large basket capitals of the half columns on the north and south walls. The height of the façades, the placing and the shape of the upper windows over the eastern gallery, and the arched frieze are in fact strangely reminiscent of the Cistercian monastery church at Lehnin, in Brandenburg (founded 1180), so meticulously analyzed by Richard Hamann. As a matter of fact, Chernigov had more or less direct contacts with the West in the twelfth century through its temporary control of the western border principality of Volhynia, and the early transmission of German elements to this area is therefore not surprising. As is the case with St Sophia in Kiev, the baptistry of this church occupies the southeast corner of the narthex; only here have some remnants of early frescoes been discovered.

Returning now to Kiev, the next mediaeval church to draw our attention dates from some forty years after the erection of St Sophia and departs appreciably from the latter in design and decoration. This is the Cathedral of the Assumption of the Virgin in the Crypt Monastery (figure 11). The monastery in question owes its name to the fact that its first inmates lived in crypts hollowed out of the limestone bluffs a short distance south of Kiev. The crypts are still accessible, and, now lighted by electricity, form a cool retreat on a hot August day. As the young ascetic community increased in numbers in the last quarter of the eleventh century, more imposing edifices were erected on the surface, and the Cathedral of the Assumption was thus begun in 1073. Consecrated in 1089, it was seriously damaged by fire in 1484 and 1718, reconstructed in its later aspect between 1720 and 1730, and all but destroyed in the Second World War. Its exterior thus represented the ornate Ukrainian style of the early eighteenth century, and a notion of its primitive appearance could be gained only from the side of the apses (figure 12). Though the ground plan of the Assumption (figure 13) resembles in proportions that of the Transfiguration in Chernigov, there were certain significant deviations in execution. Here it should be noted that the lateral aisles were added at the moment of reconstruction in the eighteenth century, together with the cupolas at the corners of the structure and also at the front and back of the central cupola. The church originally had but one cupola placed over the central square, with six internal masonry piers, and thus offers a starting point for the single-domed church of fairly simple design which became the standard type for church architecture in the principalities of the northeast (Vladimir and Suzdal). Of the three apses of the Assumption the central one was semi-circular and the two lateral ones polygonal, a feature which immediately stands out as a distinct innovation. The church was built by Greek artisans hired from Byzantium. These experts brought with them ideas of internal decoration varying somewhat from the convention prevailing in St Sophia. While the Assumption, like St Sophia, had a mosaic of the Pantocrator in the dome and one of the Virgin in the conch of the altar apse with the Eucharist below, the inner walls of the church were frescoed with representations of the high festivals of the church, while on the piers were depicted the figures of those saints whose relics were inclosed within the walls.

Slightly younger than the Church of the Assumption in the Crypt Monastery is the Church of St Michael with the Golden Roof in the monastery of the same name, situated on the edge of the bluff overlooking the Dnieper, about five hundred yards northeast of the square upon which the church-yard of St Sophia faces (figure 14). This church was begun in 1108; the date of its completion is unknown, and the great plans for a new central plaza in Kiev involved its destruction. Like St Sophia and the Assumption, its modern excrescences are so elaborate as to make its mediaeval aspect determinable only with difficulty. As may be seen from the ground plan,

however, it was primitively conceived as a single-domed
church with three apses and six internal piers. St Michael's
departs from the Assumption in that the two lateral apses and
their corresponding naves are proportionately much narrower
than is the case in the latter church. This feature doubtless
suggested to the reconstructors of the eighteenth century the
addition of two new lateral apses of the same width as the
central one. The reconstruction also entailed the addition of
two ornate staircase housings at the front, rounded chapels
at all four corners, and characteristic buttresses to support the
extended side walls and the weight of the six new cupolas.
The interior of the original church was already rather
encumbered and darkened by the massive supporting piers,
and the modern additions did not help the plan. The Patriarch Paul of Antioch, who visited Kiev in the latter part of
the seventeenth century, has left a description of this church
before its reconstruction, from which we learn that it possessed the conventional mosaics of the Pantocrator in the
central cupola and of the Virgin Orante in the conch of the
altar apse. Below the Virgin appeared in mosaic the Eucharist
and the Fathers of the Church, while the remainder of the
church was adorned with frescoes. The only extant mediaeval
decorations are the mosaic of the Eucharist (figure 15), a
figure of St Thomas, fragments of three other apostles, and
single figures of St Demetrius of Thessalonica and St Stephen.
The Eucharist is of special interest for its deviation from the
treatment exemplified in the corresponding mosaic of St
Sophia. The mosaics in St Michael's are attributed to a
native Russian artist, Olympius, a gifted inmate of the Crypt
Monastery, who learned his technique from the Greek masters engaged for the adornment of the Cathedral of the

Assumption in his own cloister. It was long customary for Russian critics to place the Eucharist of St Michael's on a lower artistic level than that in St Sophia. With regard to the actual mechanical execution this opinion is perhaps justified, since the stock of colors is less varied, and the work of setting lacks the dexterity and refinement of the Greek masters. On the other hand, the Russian artist's conception of the figures themselves gives proof of a fine originality which confers a special merit upon his work. The apostles in the mosaic of St Michael's lack the ceremonial formality which characterizes their portraits in St Sophia; their figures are more varied, their gestures more lively, their facial impressions more diversified. Even the angels bearing flabella who stand behind the communion table share the vitality of the other participants in the sacred scene. This scene is set against a golden ground, but the artist apparently made an effort to diminish the sharp contrasts between the brighter colors which he used for the garments of the apostles. Brown and crimson tones thus do not occur in close proximity to each other, but are separated by appreciable intervals. The Eucharist of St Michael's may be rightly classed as one of the finest examples of mediaeval Russian church decoration.

The last of the great churches of Kiev is that of the Holy Trinity in the monastery of St Cyril. This retreat was founded in the northern suburbs of Kiev in 1140 by Prince Vsevolod of Chernigov to commemorate his accession to the principality, and was subsequently completed by his wife. The institution ceased to be used as a monastery in 1787, when it was transformed into a veteran's home. It is now an insane asylum. The important frescoes in the monastery church were whitewashed over and forgotten until their rediscovery toward the end of the last century. The ground plan of St Cyril's is practically identical with that of St Michael's. It thus repeats the basic features of one cupola and six massive interior masonry piers, set in a somewhat elongated rectangle terminating at the east in three semi-circular apses. Exterior views of the monastery show the characteristic features of eighteenth-century reconstruction, with new cupolas of the Western type surmounted by lanterns and the small cupolas at the corners which were, of course, not a feature of the church as originally constructed in the twelfth century.

What is particularly interesting about St Cyril's is not its ground plan or its exterior, but the scheme of the interior decoration, which is particularly diversified and extensive. It comprises scenes from the Apocalypse, the life of Christ, the career of the Virgin, and the biography of the patron of the monastery, St Cyril of Alexandria, the patriarch of the fourth century to whose bigotry the assassination of Hypatia is sometimes attributed. The whole scheme of decoration shows the old conventions of arrangement as typi-fied in St Sophia combined with certain obvious modifications produced by contemporary taste. As usual, the conch of the altar portrayed the Virgin Intercessor with Eucharist and Church Fathers below. Below the cupola on the south side appeared the Nativity, on the pillars of the altar arch Christ in the temple and the Crucifixion, and on the arch itself the Annunciation. A novel feature of the religious portraiture in this church is the number of figures of Balkan Slavic saints, which point to intimate early relations between this monastery and the institutions of Mt Athos. Certain of the saintly figures depicted seem to be copies from twelfth-century

Byzantine originals provided with Russian inscriptions. Such is particularly the case with the frescoes in the sanctuary of St Cyril. In calm and symmetrical forms, and with a formal immobility entirely characteristic of Byzantine art of the twelfth century, these figures are flat and the accessories mostly without perspective. The fresco of Cyril instructing the emperor is interesting for its portrayal of Byzantine imperial costume: the emperor (figure 16) wears a jewelled stemma on his head, a sort of shoulder cape with a flap hanging down over the chest, both decorated with jewels, a dark red outer garment edged with green, and red leather boots decorated with pearls. This picture typifies St Cyril's epistle on the faith addressed to the Emperor Theodosius. In the second fresco (figure 17) Cyril is writing a religious tract while two of his subordinates peep timidly through the door in pious admiration. The frescoes of St Cyril's have suffered appreciably from unscientific restoration work executed in the '80's and cannot be appraised with entire justice from their present aspect.

Leaving St Sophia apart as a monument unique in conception and design, we thus see from this examination of the early Kievan structures that in the twelfth century the churches of South Russia crystallized into the single-domed, six-column type based on the Byzantine four-pier or four-column church. The individuality of the twelfth-century South Russian designers lies chiefly in their deviation from the norm of interior decoration set by Byzantine convention in the ninth century. In the next chapter, we shall follow the track of Byzantine influence northward to Novgorod, where we shall observe not only the transmission of the Kievan style, but also striking innovations, first in the interior decoration, and later, in churches of the twelfth and thirteenth centuries, in the actual construction, particularly of the apses, as efforts were made to adapt their treatment to the more rigorous northern climate. In northern churches of the fourteenth century, we shall also notice the reflex of early Renaissance influences transmitted through Byzantium, and, in Pskov particularly, find traces of German influence in the treatment of the roof and the decoration of the façade.

*   *   *

2. Novgorod and Pskov

2. Novgorod and Pskov

WHILE discussing the chief churchly edifices at Kiev, we noticed that the original aspect of practically every one of them had been seriously altered by reconstructions executed at the close of the seventeenth century. The two cities which now engage our attention offer in contrast a considerable number of early churches preserved substantially as they appeared when first erected. This preservation is due primarily to the geographical situation of Novgorod and its dependent territory. The city lies almost at the mediaeval northern border of Slavic settlement. It was thus far beyond the reach of the nomad hordes who so often menaced Kiev in the twelfth century, and Novgorod even escaped the bitterest manifestations of the Tartar supremacy.

Novgorod itself was in regular and constant touch with Byzantium. In the twelfth century, companies of merchants from Novgorod made the journey down the Dnieper to the Black Sea and Constantinople, including in their caravans many pious pilgrims on their way either to the monasteries of the Greek Empire or to the hallowed spots of the Holy Land. It is about the same time that relations between Novgorod and the West became more intense. From the twelfth to the sixteenth century, the Baltic was a Hanseatic lake. Merchants from Lübeck established a post at Visby, on the island of Gotland, toward the close of the eleventh century; in 1160 they founded Riga at the mouth of the Dvina, and in 1285 Reval, the capital of modern Esthonia, joined the Hanseatic League. Before 1200, Hanseatic merchants had begun to settle in Novgorod, where they soon established permanent residences fitted up as armed blockhouses to withstand the sometimes unwelcome attentions of a turbulent native population. The foreign commerce of Novgorod over the Baltic was thus handled by Hanseatic representatives. The native merchants limited themselves to gathering domestic products for export and to the distribution of imported Western goods—chiefly grains, metals, and textiles. We may accordingly expect to find in the architecture of Novgorod some mixture of Byzantine and German style, though the prestige of Kiev, the authority of Byzantium, and the piety of the Orthodox ensure the domination of the former.

The social and political organization of Novgorod in its prime was unique among Russian cities and principalities. At Kiev the prince and his retainers were supreme. At Novgorod the prince played a minor role, being pushed into the background by the local burgomaster, who was elected by an assembly of all the citizens. The inhabitants of Novgorod were inordinately jealous of their democratic privileges and collisions between the wealthy nobles and patrician merchants were frequent. Novgorod reached its prime after the Tartar invasion and the fall of Kiev—from 1240 forward. Pskov, the chief vassal city of Novgorod, became independent in 1348, but the colonizing and mercantile influence of Novgorod extended all over Northern Russia to the White Sea and even to northwestern Siberia. The decline of Novgorod dates from the middle of the fifteenth century, when social disorders become peculiarly acute. The prosperity of Novgorod was also a thorn in the side of the ambitious princes of Moscow, who were able to throttle it by their control of the southern grain supply. In 1478, Ivan III of Moscow finally had himself recognized as sovereign of the old republic. In 1495, the agencies of the Hanseatic merchants were pillaged, and in 1570 the economic life of mediaeval Novgorod came to an end when Ivan the Terrible caused most of the local population to be either massacred or deported.

At its inception, the prevailing architecture of Novgorod is simpler than that of Kiev and less ornate in its evolution than either the contemporary style of Vladimir and Suzdal in the east or the elaborate decorations of subsequent Muscovite taste. As a middle-class republic, Novgorod made no pretense to the aristocratic splendors of Kiev. Its churches are thus small, sometimes rather stumpy and close to the ground, and frequently so modest in decoration as to appear almost beggarly. Furthermore, the severe climate and heavy snowfall of this northern area inspire certain architectural modifications of the Byzantine tradition. Roofs become steeper in slope, lateral apses are absorbed into the east wall, flat dome profiles are replaced by the characteristic onion shape which appears at Novgorod for the first time. At the same time, the gabled roofs and corbel-table ornament so frequently encountered on Novgorodian churches are an obvious reflex of German influence.

As is the case in Kiev, the architectural history of Novgorod begins with the unique monument of which the design, though imitated in detail, is never duplicated in full. This is the Cathedral of St Sophia (figures 18-23), constructed between 1045 and 1052 to replace a wooden church of the same name destroyed by fire in the former year (suggested earlier as the source of inspiration for the thirteen original cupolas on St Sophia in Kiev). St Sophia in Novgorod, constructed of local grayish-yellow stone with intervening courses of fine brick, is an augmented example of the four-column church of the inscribed-cross type. The cathedral was not stuccoed externally until 1152. It has, however, only three apses (the two semicircular projections at the northeast and southeast corners are one-story chapels) and five cupolas, exclusive of that surmounting the staircase tower of the west façade. The arcades on south, west and north seem to have been added to the original structure (figure 19) soon after its erection, if we may judge from the inclusion in the western arcade of the staircase tower (figures 20, 22), which stood free, like the original tower of the church of the Transfiguration at Chernigov. Originally, St Sophia was thus also a church of the six-column type. Apart from an extra chapel added to the east end in the sixteenth century, St Sophia in Novgorod presents substantially its primitive aspect after the addition of the lateral extensions. In 1893 an excellent job of renovation entailed rebuilding one entire wall, but the original lines of the church were not violated in the process.

However interesting architecturally, St Sophia is by no means one of the most imposing Russian churches, nor is its decoration to be classed as rich. The dimensions of the primitive structure without arcades were forty-eight feet in width by eighty-one feet in length, the main cupola being one hundred eight feet high. It was built before the commercial supremacy and wealth of Novgorod had reached its zenith, and therefore reflects the as yet modest economic status of the city while it was still the chief northern tributary of Kiev.

An expedient of early French Romanesque churches here

reproduced is the use of a quadrant vault to connect the walls of the outer aisles with those of the central naves. The transverse aisles are covered with a series of semicircular and pointed roofs, of which the latter are faced with sheets of slate, of a type unparalleled in Byzantine practice. The lateral apses are rounded and the central one is polygonal. None of them is decorated with niches, but a notable feature is the height of the lateral apses, which approximates that of the central one, and all three are substantially of the same height as the naves in order to support the thrust of the five cupolas. The flat walls of the side arcades spaced with pilaster strips have an archaic Romanesque aspect, and the decoration at the eaves around the domes of the cupolas, resembling similar features on the cathedral at Worms, together with the lisenes on the central apse, confirm this impression.

While the exterior thus has a distinct Romanesque aspect, the interior (figure 21), with its massive columns, is immediately reminiscent of St Sophia in Kiev. Galleries mounted on arches surround the three sides opposite the apses. The central apse is decorated to about six feet from the floor with mosaic panels of rich geometrical design. The walls were originally frescoed throughout, but of these decorations little is preserved except the Pantocrator in the main cupola and the more recently discovered figures of the prophets in the drum. The frescoes in general have suffered severely from unskilled restorations which have largely destroyed their original character. The fresco of the Pantocrator in the cupola has the right hand raised but closed. To this fresco is attached the legend that the painters vainly tried three times to represent Christ's hand opened in blessing, and three times it was miraculously closed; the third time they heard a mysterious voice saying that the clenched hand enclosed the destiny of Novgorod, which should not fall till it was opened. As far as can be judged from the scanty remains discovered, the arrangement of the frescoes corresponds to the Byzantine convention observed by the eleventh-century school of Kiev.

Before leaving St Sophia we should notice its two sets of bronze doors, which by their character typify the duality of influence which governed its conception. The so-called Sigtuna doors, named for a Swedish city pillaged in 1187, but actually having no connection with it, show a design of Italo-Byzantine ornamental character, the technique of which is paralleled, for example, at Amalfi, Salerno, and Venice, and at Rome in the doors of St Paul's outside the Walls. The so-called Khersonian doors, on the west front (figure 23), which tradition reported to have been brought from Kherson in the Crimea by St Vladimir, are actually of much later date and have nothing whatever to do with Kherson. They have been most recently studied in detail by Professor Gold-schmidt. They are actually Saxon work of the middle twelfth century, having been made in Magdeburg about 1152. They were not cast in one piece, but consist of separate plates on a wooden backing. Beside the original Latin legends, several of the scenes have Russian labels subsequently added, a few of which indicate that the Russians did not rightly interpret the scenes depicted. The doors seem originally to have been ordered for a church in the Polish city of Polotsk, and then bought for presentation to St Sophia.

Next in antiquity to St Sophia stands the Church of St Nicholas erected in 1113 by Prince Yaroslav (figure 24). It is a simple edifice of the type with six internal columns and one cupola familiar from Kiev, but has three semicircular apses all of equal height with the corresponding naves; the apses are decorated with flat niches of the sort which appear on the apses of St Sophia in Kiev. The round cupola has only four windows, like the side cupolas of St Sophia in Novgorod, and the church, when viewed from the apses, presents a rather striking similarity to the central part of the east end of the latter. As a matter of fact, St Nicholas gives an excellent idea how the standard Kievan six-pillar churches (e.g., the Assumption and St Michael's) must have looked before their modern excrescences were added. Very little of the primitive decoration of this church is preserved.

A church of almost identical antiquity and design with St Nicholas is that of St George in the monastery of the same name, built in 1119 and partly ruined in the late war (figure 25). Here again we have the six-pillar type with three semicircular apses of equal height with the naves. St George's differs from St Nicholas', however, in that there is a transept in front of the sanctuary, which pushes the cupola further forward than is the case either in St Nicholas' or in the Assumption in the Crypt Monastery. This feature also characterizes the previously mentioned Transfiguration at Chernigov. The church has two smaller cupolas over at the west end, and a tower at the northwest corner copied from St Sophia. The high and massive silhouette of St George's and the lines of the massive apses unrelieved by niches or windows show that it proceeds from the same school as St Sophia itself. The same decorative pattern is used on the cupolas as on those of the latter building. The system of two cupolas and a tower has certain analogies with Greek churches, especially that of 1028 dedicated to the Virgin in Salonika. The apsidal forms are also a direct importation from Constantinople and corroborate the tradition of direct intercourse between Novgorod and Byzantium. The mural decorations of St George's have all been modernized.

Modifications in the design of these almost monotonously box-like structures begin to appear in the second half of the twelfth century. These changes affect most prominently the handling of the apses; the two lateral ones descend below the level of the altar apse and become little more than one-story projections. At the same time the number of internal columns is reduced to four which support the single cupola. These phases are well-exemplified by the Church of the Redeemer at Nereditsa (outside Novgorod), built in 1197 and a total casualty in the Second World War. Here at one time in the church's history the whole structure was topped with a four-sloped roof (figure 26), which doubtless caught less snow than the primitive curves (figure 27). The influence of St Sophia is again noticeable in the decorative line around the cupola, and the arrangement of the bricks to line the inside of the external arches shows traces of Western European practice.

This church was of peculiar importance because the murals were preserved. The extent of the wall space was here particularly favorable to a complex decorative scheme. Since this church was really dedicated to the Ascension, the conventional Pantocrator of the Kievan cupolas is here replaced by a mural of the Ascension. Christ here mounts to heaven seated on a rainbow, holding the book of seven seals in his hand and supported by six angels. The apostles watch his departure. In the drum below the prophets unroll scrolls announcing his first coming, and the four evangelists occupy the pendentives.

In the altar apse were placed the Virgin Intercessor (figure 28), with the Eucharist below. To these decorations of the altar space were added scenes depicting two Old Testament precursors of the Eucharist: Abraham's entertainment of the three angels and Elijah fed by ravens. There is one distinction to be drawn here between the representation of Christ as priest (figure 29) in the church at Nereditsa and the one in St Sophia at Kiev. At Nereditsa, Christ appeared as priest in the lower row of figures in the altar apse, while in St Sophia at Kiev the figure is in a medallion high above the altar arch. The figure at Nereditsa closely resembled that at Kiev in convention, but already reflects the somber, even somewhat threatening expression characterizing twelfth-century representations. The church also contained a fresco of the Last Judgment with elements known in the Caucasus but not in Byzantium. This and other Oriental reminiscences are explicable by the fact that Prince Yaroslav, the builder of this church, possessed close contacts with the Caucasus through his wife. His relations with Western Europe were also intimate, since he was the first prince of Novgorod to sign a treaty with the Germans in 1199. Among the frescoes representing scenes from the life of Christ was an interesting depiction of his baptism (figure 30). A reflex of Western influence is traceable in the processions of saints at either side of the Virgin in the altar apse. Here Byzantine convention tolerated only archangels, but such saintly processions are characteristic of early Romanesque art. In the southern lunette next to the entrance door was a very interesting picture of Prince Yaroslav, the builder, offering a model of the church to a seated Christ. An inscription explains the scene, which was obviously suggested by similar Byzantine representations. This was, with one exception, the oldest portrait of a Russian prince.

The frescoes of Nereditsa, though much praised and extremely popular, were of only limited artistic value. They had no local character and were simply monuments of Byzantine art transplanted to Russia. The coloring was unimpressive, being a dull complex of ochres and browns unrelieved by brighter hues. These frescoes still preserved the style of the mosaic for which they are a substitute: single figures predominate, and groups are relatively less common.

Toward the beginning of the thirteenth century, the architects of Novgorod continued to modify still further their more or less cubical basic design as exemplified in the churches we have just examined in search of better adaptation to northern climatic conditions. The roof of the churches, instead of being constructed as a four-sloped cap over the tops of the arches, such as we saw on the church at Nereditsa prior to its restoration, is sometimes replaced by an eight-sloped roof with four gables, and at the same time, the lateral apses containing *prothesis* and *diakonikon* disappear from the exterior of the church altogether, being replaced by recesses in the eastern wall or other internal arrangements. Though the transition to this type appears as early as 1156, it is most fully developed in the fourteenth century. Some churches of this class, as we shall see in a moment, were constructed with two or three vestibules, the idea of which is traceable to the Caucasus or Asia Minor, but these vestibules were subsequently omitted in the more impressive churches of this period.

An example of this type of church, except in respect to the roof, on which the original four gables have been eliminated by early reconstruction, is that of St Nicholas built in 1292 at Lipno, not far from Novgorod (figure 31). It is a cubical church with four internal columns and one very small apse, roughly only half the height of the east wall. The external treatment of the façade is somewhat novel. There is no effort to indicate the interior arrangement of the church. At each corner is a pilaster from which a line of decoration rises to a triple arch in the center providing the transition to the cupola. The cupola itself is girdled by a small Romanesque pattern, and small arches in relief appear over the windows. The west façade shows blind windows, two larger ones in the center, and two narrower ones near the extremities. The frescoes of this church are lost. Drawings made toward the middle of the last century show that they comprised a Pantocrator in the cupola, figures of the prophets on the walls between the windows, and a Last Judgment on the west wall. The two best-preserved figures are representations of the sainted princes Boris and Gleb.

To the type of single-apse church belong two others of somewhat later date; the Church of the Redeemer in Kovalyovo, built in 1345, thus shows three vestibules, though the roof preserved the four-slope type (figure 32), while the Church of the Transfiguration in Volotovo (1352) has only two vestibules. This latter church is of singular importance for its frescoes. It was now over a century since intellectual and artistic life had ceased in Southern Russia with the onslaught of the Tartars, but Novgorod was at its zenith of commercial prosperity. While economically Novgorod was doubtless oriented toward the West, its ecclesiastical and therefore its cultural connections with Byzantium remained intimate during the last two centuries of the Eastern Empire,

a period which is characterized by what is known as the
Byzantine Renaissance under the Palaeologi, the contemporary Greek ruling house. Entire agreement does not prevail
among specialists as to the proportion of Western increments
in this new productive period of mediaeval Greek art. The
fact remains, however, that since the Crusades the contacts
of Byzantium with Italy, and particularly with Venice, had
taken on a new intensity, so that influence in both directions
is by no means unlikely, even if one does not accept the
theory of complete Byzantine dependence on Italian monuments of the *Trecento*. It is difficult to brush aside the
observation that to the noble traditions of Hellenistic protrai-
ture, the Byzantine artists of this period added new notions
of perspective and a fresh naturalism in interpretation which
were characteristic of Italian Renaissance art. At any rate,
it is the new type of Greek art originating under the Palaeologi
which is reflected in the frescoes at Volotovo. The similarity
of style between the frescoes in the church of the Transfiguration at Volotovo and the mosaics in the mosque of
Qahriye-jami at Constantinople is frequently so striking that
the Byzantine influence is undeniable, and when the two
series deviate, this dissimilarity is frequently traceable to
Italian influences current in Byzantium itself.

The frescoes in the church at Volotovo have a dual character. One part is comparable with the archaic tradition of
the Byzantine period of the Palaeologi in severe iconographic
style and flat linear execution. This earlier section is typified
by the two angelic figures (figure 33) in the composition
of the Eucharist standing beside the altar with the chalice
which bore the Christ child—a novel motive for the period.
Their conception is more active and more vitalized than in

early paintings. Yet their icon-like style is manifest in the uniform vertical lines of their robes, and in the linear drawing of the heads. The later frescoes show a completely different character, much more lively and complex than the restrained and formal manner of earlier work. In this new manner, the sharp outlines and the linear style have given way to spots of color, distribution of light and shade, and accentuation of the relief of the figures. Heads, faces, and garments are in uniform tints, but relief is represented by prominent bits of coloring or dark shadows. The eyes, for example, are not defined by heavy lines, but expressed by deep shadows, with a spot of white representing the white of the eye. The static saints of the eleventh century begin to move, to turn their heads and bodies in various directions. The soldiers incline their spears in warlike readiness or brandish their swords. A new movement enters compositions of the Transfiguration, the Descent into Hell, and the Annunciation. In this renewed vitality speaks the spirit of the Renaissance as transmitted to Novgorod through Byzantine channels. While the subjects of the frescoes remain substantially the same, they become less abstract. The Pantocrator in the cupola is transformed into the Messiah descending to earth, the Virgin Intercessor in the altar apse is now replaced by the Queen of Heaven, enthroned between two archangels. The Annunciation is no longer depicted on the pillars of the altar arch but at Volotovo takes its place among the scenes from the life of Christ. An original feature also presents itself in the shift of the Passion from the central section of the church to a position in the altar apse where it immediately adjoins the Eucharist, in which Christ offers the bread not to St Peter but to Judas Iscariot, who had been conventionally omitted from the older representations of the scene, more hierarchical in conception.

A very characteristic example of the second manner in the frescoes at Volotovo is the scene of the Nativity (figure 35). This fresco is adapted to a semicircular wall space. The Virgin reclines at the left beside the cradle, balanced on the opposite side by the midwife holding the infant while a maid brings water for his bath. The sheep of the fold are shown above, and three angels look down upon the whole scene. While the old sharpness of line is evident in the head-coverings of the principal figures, their attitudes and gestures are already in the free style of the Renaissance. The mountain landscape takes up more than half of the background. There was no room for Joseph in this picture, so he is depicted in the arch of the lunette (figure 34), and opposite him are seen the Three Kings. The motion in this last picture is to be noted, likewise the cloaks of the riders billowing out in the wind. These frescoes are very likely the work of a Greek artist named Theophanes, who is known to have worked in both Novgorod and Moscow toward the close of the fourteenth century. His influence on Muscovite art was considerable.

Two other churches in Novgorod itself give a somewhat better idea of the handling of the eight-slope roofs as an innovation. The first of these, the Church of St Theodore Stratilates (the General) (figure 36), was built in 1361. Here you have reproduced the general type of the Church of St. Nicholas, but with more complex treatment of apse and façades.

The lateral façades here have two inner pilasters beside those at the corners, and over the center is a trifoliate arch, while the arches over the side pilasters also have two corresponding subdivisions. The apse is decorated with arcades at the middle and a series of niches above, with decorative handling of the bricks set on end under the eaves. The internal arches rest on double graduated impost blocks. The Church of the Transfiguration in Novgorod (figure 37), which was built only fourteen years after St Theodore's, shows such close agreement with the former as to lead to the supposition that it was erected by the same group of builders. The Transfiguration shows one detail omitted from St Theodore's: a Romanesque entrance with multiple profiled arches. The cupolas are almost identical in decoration, and are slender enough to possess considerable grace.

Though politically and historically dependent upon Novgorod and sharing in general the artistic progress of the metropolis, Pskov shows some interesting architectural innovations. Here too we find German influences in roof treatment and façade decoration, but primitively the Kievan forms dominate here as in Novgorod. In the later Middle Ages, the architects of Pskov enjoyed a high reputation, and their talents were employed on Moscow construction projects of the fifteenth century.

The first church in Pskov which deviates sensibly from the Kiev pattern is that of the Transfiguration in the Mirozhski Monastery, built in 1156. It is built of local stone, and presents the familiar cubical lines, with a single unusually large cupola supported on four internal columns. As a matter of fact, this church was originally not cubical, but cross-shaped, and has been filled out by additions at the southwest and northwest corners over the small arch. Primitively it thus resembled St Theodore's in Athens. From east to west the church is considerably foreshortened, with only a narrow space between the altar arch and the easternmost columns under the cupola, so that the latter is off center and rather nearer the apses than in any other church we have observed. There is a narthex across the western façade. This church has three apses. As in the Church of the Redeemer at Nereditsa, the lateral apses are reduced proportionally, being only half the height of the central one; figure 38 shows the northern façade. It is to be observed that the cupola has eight windows and carries the familiar Romanesque decoration at the top of the dome. The internal arrangement is reflected in the asymmetrical blind arches of the north and south façades. The excrescence at the right is a primitive type of belfry characteristic of Pskov. The bells in these frames were rung by swinging, as in Western Europe, though in most Russian churches the bells are fixed and rung by moving the clapper.

The second church at Pskov which we shall look at is that of St John the Baptist, built in 1240 (figure 39). If one disregards the bell-frame on the south side and the one story vestibule on the west façade, it will be seen that, except in height, the lines of this church resemble those of St George's at Novgorod. We have the same six-column plan, though without the transept in front of the altar, so that the central cupola is brought over the middle of the church. The two smaller cupolas are over the western ante-church. The development of the three-domed church is connected with the usage of erecting altars to individual saints and having a cupola for each such altar. There is one interesting feature of the interior of this church which might be mentioned, viz., that of the six masonry columns, only the two eastern ones next to the altar are square, and the other four round, with rectangular impost blocks. The structural material of this church is somewhat unique. It is built of quarried blocks of local stone separated by rows of quadrangular bricks made of clay not native to Pskov and of a different color from that customary in this area, but notably resembling Dutch and English brick. The brick thus seems to have been imported.

The later Church of St Sergius (figure 40), built in the fourteenth century, shows some analogies with churches in Novgorod like St Theodore's and the Transfiguration, though without the eight-sloped roof. It is of the four-column type with graceful central cupola. While here three apses are preserved, the central one has been widened and then short-ened to a little over half the height of the east wall, while the lateral apses join it to the corners of the church. Notice the lace-like decoration on cupola and central apse; this is reproduced on St Basil's (figure 41) of the fourteenth cen-tury, which exhibits considerable affinity with St Sergius' in the treatment of the apses, which also has the north and south vestibules familiar from Volotovo and Kovalyovo.

In any discussion of the outstanding characteristics of the architecture of Novgorod, the question of the origin of the familiar onion-shaped cupola immediately presents itself. The exact date of this innovation is uncertain, but we shall see in a moment that it is possible to fix with some accuracy the approximate date at which it came into fashion. In any case, it is to be supposed that all cupolas built before 1250 were originally crowned with the flat-curved or hemispherical roof cap of more or less Byzantine type. Since this covering was not practical in a region of heavy snow, it has been urged that a natural substitute was readily found in a feature of Russian native wooden architecture, viz., the gable with onion-shaped section. Mediaeval Russian carpenters designed these roofs by drawing a circle and removing at the bottom a segment equal to a third or a fifth of its diameter, then adding this amount to the height of the roof above the upper arc of the circle. Slightly concave or straight lines were then drawn in to connect the peak with the circumference of the circle. According to the length of the segment cut out, the outline would be more or less bulbous. Some investigators have thus held that this section was used for the silhouette of the cupolas, first in polygonal, then in circular form.

This theory is not altogether satisfactory, nor has it been generally accepted. Other archaeologists have thus suggested that the pointed shape was secured by simply raising the point at which the central cross was set on each cupola, with the result that the descending lines from this peak were lengthened and curved in a way from which the onion silhouette would naturally evolve. Probably the most primitive cupola among the churches here illustrated is that which surmounts the Church of St Nicholas in Lipno, built in 1292, though an onion dome appears in a Novgorod miniature as early as 1164 (figure 42). At Lipno the central peak is only slightly raised above the surface of a fairly regular hemisphere. The next upward extension is shown by the cupolas of St George's. These cupolas are not in their primitive form, and seem to have been reconstructed toward the beginning of the thirteenth century. They not only show a distinctly higher crest than that of the cupola of St Nicholas', but the hemisphere is also slightly pinched in at the bottom, a feature which is still more noticeable on the smaller cupolas of St Sophia. Exaggeration of this pinching at the bottom, combined with a gradual lengthening of the line from the pinch to the greatest diameter of the bulb as well as with a continued raising of the peak, results very easily and naturally in the onion silhouette. The disappearance of the early flat or hemispherical cupolas is readily explained by the frequent fires in Novgorod, since the local cupolas were all mounted on wooden beams and were probably covered with slates. As a matter of fact, St Sophia was seriously damaged by fire on five separate and distinct mediaeval occasions. In view of the probability that the bulbous cupola began to achieve popularity in the second half of the thirteenth century, it is likely that the central cupola of St Sophia in Novgorod (which is the least bulbous) took its present shape in 1261, in which year we know that the Bishop Dalmatius roofed the cathedral with lead, and, as the chronicles say, thus erected to himself a monument for the ages. The cupola of the staircase tower probably dates from slightly after 1394, when it was damaged by fire; like the small cupolas, it has a bulbous form further evolved than the central one, due to a more pronounced pinch at the bottom.

Apart from this evolution of the cupola, which is doubtless the most striking innovation traceable to Novgorod, the northern metropolis, as we have seen from the examples, made another important contribution to Russian church architecture in the development of the cubical four-column church from the six-column type which prevailed in Kiev. This type was also widely adopted in the eastern principality of Vladimir-Suzdal, where it is exemplified by two of the most graceful churches of the twelfth century, that of the Transfiguration at Pereyaslavl Zalesski and the church of the Virgin Intercessor on the Nerl, both of which present, however, the vaulted roof familiar from the Church of the Redeemer at Nereditsa. Two other characteristic features of the Novgorod style, viz., the four-gabled roof and the reduction of the lateral apses, were not taken up elsewhere except at Pskov. And finally, Novgorod is particularly interesting for its adoption of Western motifs of external decoration along with its preservation of the Byzantine traditions of fresco painting as practised first in the style of the eleventh and twelfth and later in that of the fourteenth century.

In the next chapter we shall deal with the monuments of the third center of early mediaeval Russian culture, the principality of Vladimir-Suzdal, situated slightly to the northeast of modern Moscow. This principality rises to prominence in the twelfth century and gradually usurps the prestige of Kiev. The architects of Vladimir copy the second Kiev school, e.g., the lines of the Cathedral of the Assumption in the Crypt Monastery, and add new elements of Western origin which give the early churches of the northeast as distinctive a style as the modest square-cut edifices of Novgorod, and one coupled with a wealth of decoration which foreshadows the exuberant fancy of mediaeval Moscow.

* * *

3. Vladimir-Suzdal

3. Vladimir · Suzdal

W E HAVE examined briefly the types of church architecture prevalent at both ends of the Dnieper trade-route, first in Kiev, then in Novgorod. We noted that in Kiev the prevalent type of church was the six-column basilica with three naves and a single cupola, a type which is repeated in Novgorod, though often with two additional cupolas at the narthex end. We also remarked the popularity in Novgorod of the simple church with four internal columns supporting a single central cupola, and noticed the development of the four-gable roof with a considerable increment of Western decorative elements on both apses and façades. Now we turn to a third center of mediaeval Russian political and intellectual life, the principality of Vladimir-Suzdal, which first rose to prime importance toward the middle of the twelfth century after the decline of Kiev had already set in. This principality is of special interest because it includes most of the area later to form the Grand Duchy of Moscow and the nucleus of the modern Russian state, i.e., the country extending southwestward from the Volga to the headwaters of the rivers Dnieper and Desna.

The prehistoric home of the Slavs was in a rough quadrangle between the middle Vistula and the middle Dnieper. In the eastern division of this region lived the forefathers of the modern Russians. They colonized not only north-eastward in the direction of Novgorod and southeastward down the Dnieper, but also in a more generally easterly direction toward the Volga. Here they came into contact with an older stratum of scattered Finnish settlers whom they either absorbed or displaced. Indeed, as a result of this intermixture, many of the physical characteristics of the so-called Great Russians are more Finnish than Slavic. But at any rate, from the earliest period of Russian history there were, in the area which now concerns us, Slavic settlements which eventually coalesce into the principality of Vladimir-Suzdal. Of the two cities Suzdal is the older, and was probably colonized from Novgorod. Distant 33 kilometers from Suzdal and 171 kilometers from Moscow by rail is the city of Vladimir, now chiefly celebrated for its textile industry, but actually founded by Prince Vladimir Monomakh early in the twelfth century. Until nearly 1100, this whole region was a sparsely settled area like modern Siberia, a paradise for hunters and trappers. It first takes on political importance in 1097 when Suzdal was organized as a principality and assigned to Vladimir Monomakh, later prince of Kiev (1113-1125), one of the most distinguished figures in early Russian history. He later allotted it as a domain to his youngest son Yuri Dolgoruki (George Longarm), who died in 1157. During the first half of the twelfth century, a large number of new towns were laid out and largely populated by refugees from the southern part of the Kiev districts where nomad forays were at this period rapidly destroying all bases of an ordered existence. Among the towns thus founded were Moscow itself, as yet an unimportant border fortress and hunting lodge, and Yuryev Polski (literally 'Georgetown in the Clearing') named for Prince George, Tver, now on the railroad line between Moscow and Leningrad, and Kostroma on the Volga. Yuri's constructive work was continued by his son Andrew (known as Andrei Bogolyubski, from his favorite residence at the town of Bogolyubovo), who was assassinated in 1175, and by Andrew's younger brother Vsevolod. It is with these three princes of the twelfth century that the chief edifices which we shall examine are to be associated.

While relations between Novgorod and Vladimir were always close, the twelfth and early thirteenth-century structures now under consideration were all erected before the characteristic northern innovations were carried through at Novgorod. Hence the dominating influences will be Kiev and Byzantium. On the other hand, we shall have occasion to see that even in this apparently remote district Western influences also made themselves felt. We have direct historical evidence as to the Kievan influences, since a mediaeval Russian source reports that Vladimir Monomakh had measures taken of the Cathedral of the Assumption in the Crypt Monastery at Kiev in order to duplicate it in a church at the old city of Rostov, also in the northeast, and it is specifically stated that these data were passed on to Yuri Dolgoruki, who used them as a basis for the construction of a church in Suzdal. Another important factor for the development of northeastern architecture was the presence of a good supply of white stone comparatively near by on the Volga, which relieved the local architects of the restrictions imposed by the use of brick in Kiev. This factor also facilitated the adoption of Western forms, the passage of which to the northeast followed a route from the western principalities of Galicia and Volhynia through Chernigov; the latter city had, as we remarked in the first chapter, abundant contacts with the West Russian border, and after 1125 was fully as close to Vladimir-Suzdal politically as it was to Kiev.

The earliest church preserved among those constructed by Yuri Dolgoruki is that of Saints Boris and Gleb at Kideksha, built in 1152 about four miles from Suzdal (figure 43). The loss of its primitive roof and cupola somewhat disguises its analogies with the Church of the Assumption in the Yeletski Monastery (figure 10). Its original roof was probably vaulted like that on the Church of the Redeemer at Nereditsa, already mentioned (figures 26, 27). It is a four-column structure without narthex (the porch being modern), and shows the same belt of corbel-table ornament which we saw on the Yeletski church, only lower down. Above this is a row of brick-shaped cut stones, set with an edge to the front, which is a pronounced characteristic of Vladimir-Suzdal ornament. Like the latter church, the western façade is symmetrically divided by pilasters; the lateral façades, however, are asymmetrically divided because of the lengthwise shortening of the church. The church is built of native white stone.

The second extant church built by Yuri Dolgoruki was begun in 1152 but completed by his son Andrew in 1157, at Pereyaslavl Zalesski, north of Vladimir (figure 44). The name of the town, Pereyaslavl 'beyond the forests', to distinguish it from the city of the same name south of Kiev, reflects its settlement by colonists from the south. Here again we have a four-column church, built of white stone with one cupola and the original arched roof. This church lacks the grace and harmony of the later major structures in and about Vladimir. It is closer to the ground and more archaic than these, but is important as a prototype of subsequent structures. At the edge of the cupola is a cornice consisting of a Byzantine line of ornament with triangular points down which recurs again and again on churches of this area. The saw-tooth ornament occurs both above the corbel-tables on the three apses and above the frieze on the drum of the cupola. The apses themselves are rather of the Kievan than the Novgorodian type.

These two churches are less pretentious in conception and more modest in ornament than the churches built toward the begining of the thirtenth century and later. The ornamental forms resemble those in Chernigov. But from the capture of Constantinople by the Crusaders in 1204 and the foundation of the Latin Empire of the East, the influence of Western Europe becomes more and more marked in north-eastern Russia, though the possibility of ornamental borrowings from the Caucasus and Armenia should not be lost sight of in view of the line of communication down the Volga.

The most imposing architectural monument of north-eastern Russian art is the Cathedral of the Assumption at Vladimir, completed by Prince Andrew in 1158 (figures 45 to 49). For its construction and adornment, Andrew employed numerous foreign artisans, and for pure splendor this church was the richest and most ornate ever seen in Russia. But unfortunately most of the city of Vladimir was destroyed by fire in 1185, and the cathedral was reduced to ruins. It was thus reconstructed in subsequent years by Andrew's brother and successor Vsevolod, and reconsecrated in 1189. The basic design of this church resembles that of the Assumption at Kiev,—six columns, three apses, and one cupola. It was erected entirely from white stone brought from Bulgaria, (this may mean Kazan) instead of the Volga stone employed in the earlier churches. When Prince Vsevolod restored it, he expanded it by adding an arcade on all three sides and adding four corner cupolas (figures 46, 47), but to the credit of his artisans it must be admitted that the reconstruction is so masterly as to give the impression of a single unified structure. The curved roof of the arcades does not come quite to the height of the vaults of the main and original structure, thus supplying an extremely ingenious perspective. The cupolas, it will be noticed, are helmet-shaped, modern restorations replacing late cupolas of the bulbous type (figure 48). The decoration is distinctly more complex than in the two churches just discussed. The corbel-table line familiar from Chernigov and Novgorod has moved upward from the drum of the cupola to the base of the cupola itself. Below the rim of the cupola we find the line of vertically set stone familiar from Pereyaslavl Zalesski and below that the angular frieze also observed there. Below this frieze the corbel-table is repeated, supported by engaged colonettes with Corinthian-esque capitals, which are repeated in larger dimensions at the corners and on the pilasters of the façades (figure 49). Both windows and portals are of the Romanesque type with set-backs. The concentric arches of the portals are also supported by small columns. A few relief masks of birds and lions on the tympana beside the windows show scanty remnants of the original relief decoration, which was extensive and included various biblical and apocryphal scenes. The original polychrome character of the external walls is also indicated by some fragmentary external frescoes. A few internal fresco fragments discovered in 1918 are as yet unpublished. A very characteristic and distinctive feature of Vladimirian architecture is the row of small engaged columns supporting an arched corbel-table and moulding all around the middle of the façades. On the west façade this decoration is in relief on the wall itself. The colonettes are fully worked out with capitals and bases, the latter supported on carved consoles. This ornament is reproduced under the cornice of the apses, with some of the colonettes extending the whole height of the apse. On the lateral façades, however, where there are four blind windows; this decoration is repeated but with recesses between the pilasters. The recessed windows with multiple retreating arches have a pronounced Romanesque aspect.

The fact that the extant ornament on this cathedral even after its restoration in 1189 is very close to the original features is proved by similar characteristics which appear on the Church of the Virgin Intercessor on the river Nerl, a short distance outside Vladimir (figures 50 to 54). This veritable jewel of Russian architecture was built in 1165 of the same 'Bulgarian' stone which was employed for the Cathedral of the Assumption. With its single cupola and graceful vertical lines it must possess a great deal of the charm which surrounded the Cathedral of the Assumption in its original aspect. Here once more is a church with four columns and three apses (figure 51) which rise almost to the vaults of a roof resembling that of the church at Pereyaslavl Zalesski (figure 44). The church is, however, more oblong than square. Here again the façades are divided by half-columns with Corinthianesque capitals which are repeated at the corners. The line of decorative colonettes supporting an arched corbel-table and moulding is repeated on both façades and apses. While the bulb of the cupola is obviously not primitive, as may be inferred from the restoration of those on the Cathedral of the Assumption, the decoration on the drum is practically identical with the latter, with a corbel-table at the top, followed by a moulding, then the line of cut stone set with vertical edges out; below the latter the saw-tooth element, and finally another corbel-table supported by engaged colonettes on either side of the windows. The tympana of the windows show female masks and animal figures in relief. The central tympanum on each side shows a relief of King David (figures 52, 53) on a throne holding a seven stringed instrument in his left hand, while his right is raised in an oratorical gesture. On each side of him stands a bird with outstretched wings and a lion with waving tail, and below them three female masks, followed by two lions at either side of the window. In the side tympana are gryphons, each holding a hare between its paws and below them two female masks (figure 54). The carvings of the consoles supporting the ornamental colonettes on façades and apses are particularly interesting; in some cases conventionalized animal heads, in others female heads, and again carved eagles.

The extent of this ornamentation on the church at the Nerl is still restricted, but in the next church which we discuss it attains an exuberance totally beyond what one would expect from the rather dull exterior of many of the churches we have discussed. The Cathedral of St Dmitri, dedicated to St Demetrius of Salonika, was built by Prince Andrew's brother Vsevolod between 1193 and 1197 (figures 55-57). It follows the basic idea of the Church of the Virgin Intercessor, as a four-column structure with three apses, but gives a rather heavier impression, since the vertical lines are proportionately not so prolonged. It repeats all the familiar features of the decoration of both the churches we have just studied, but almost always with elaboration. The cap of the cupola is of the primitive flat type. It rests on a corbel-table supported by a moulding below which we have the familiar saw-tooth frieze and then the cornice of triangular points, now graduated and each adorned with a lion mask. Between the colonettes at each side of the windows of the drum is a niche filled alternately with relief heads of saints and with relief birds and animals framed with an intertwining vine relief making successive circles in vertical series. Around the middle of the façades we find the same moulding supported by colonettes which appears in the Assumption and on the church at the Nerl. The spaces between the shafts are not left blank, however, but occupied with reliefs of plants and birds, while between the capitals of the small engaged columns appear relief figures of saints, surmounted each by an animal figure, a bird, or a plant. The designers had the good sense to leave the walls below these ornaments blank, but the consoles supporting the small columns are carved with animal forms or masks. Similar motives recur on the apses.

It is in the tympana that the most striking decorations are found. The symbolism is plainly that of Psalm 148 and the *Benedicite omnia opera*, especially the latter, where various animals are called on seriatim to bless the Lord. For example, in the central tympana on the north and south fronts David is represented as on the church at the Nerl, surrounded by a whole menagerie of animals interspersed with plants and shrubs. He no longer holds a harp, however, but is preaching from a scroll. The tympana carry not only scenes from the Bible, but hagiographical elements like St Nicetas and the devil or apocryphal stories like Solomon going to heaven on a gryphon. The bizarre types of mythical animals, basilisks, dragons, and gryphons are a reflex of the mediaeval conception of the animal kingdom exhibited in the *Physiologus*. Some features remind one of similar decorations on the Cathedral of Ripoll in Catalonia, while the lions facing each other on the impost blocks of the interior can be paralleled in French Romanesque decorations.

In 1918, there were discovered in St Dmitri's some remnants of frescoes which Russian scholars consider superior to anything else of this nature which Byzantine art of the Comnencian period produced. They are part of a large composition of the Last Judgment. Details like those on figure 56 representing an Apostle, or the righteous women (figure 57), are sufficient to show their remarkable character.

The churches just described belong to a school of architects and artisans definitely associated with Andrei Bogolyubski and retaining a very distinct tradition of design, form, and decoration. Early in the thirteenth century, however, a new school rises which is even less restrained in its use of decoration. The flat reliefs of the earlier school are abandoned for more rounded sculptural forms and higher relief. This new tendency rises simultaneously with the Latin Empire at Constantinople, when the Byzantine tradition which tolerated no sculptures on the façades was weakened, and thus opened the path to Romanesque and Oriental influences which now fuse with the previous Russian forms.

The first church which reflects this change in style and taste is that of the Nativity of the Virgin in Suzdal (figure 58). A church of this name was begun by Vladimir Monomakh in 1125, and completed by his son Yuri Dolgoruki. The primitive structure was torn down in 1222 and replaced by a new edifice, which was a six-column structure with three vestibules, like some of the smaller churches in Novgorod. The new church had only one cupola, and thus reproduced the prevailing Kievan style of the previous century. One vestibule with copper doors is still extant, but in 1528 its walls were torn down to a third of their height, so that the early reliefs were largely destroyed. Only the row of ornamental colonettes and the arched corbel-table around the façades are preserved. Note that the columns rest on a projection of the wall and not on consoles, as is the case in the two churches previously described. There is no decoration in the niches between the colonettes, but the columns themselves are incised with patterns, as is the case with their capitals and bases. The presence of sculptured female masks indicates the possibility that the niches originally also contained reliefs. Here we no longer have the simple saw-tooth pattern above the corbel-table. The former is replaced by a row of cut stones or short columns carved in a pine-cone design. The moulding above is also carved. The broad pilasters are strongly profiled, and are not decorated with half-columns, as in the case of the Assumption and St Dmitri's. They are topped with an impost block faced with a slab carved with a female head in low relief. These heads are inferior in plastic effect to those on the Church of the Virgin Intercessor at the Nerl. The basket capitals of the doorways (figure 59) are an inheritance from the earlier churches.

Almost contemporary with the second church on this site is the Cathedral of St George in Yuryev Polski, erected in 1230-1234 (figure 60). This church collapsed in 1471 and was restored by order of Ivan III of Moscow. In the restoration the church was made somewhat lower, and the old reliefs were set up on the walls in hit-or-miss fashion, so that the original aspect is lost. This church is a four-column structure with three apses and three vestibules. The roof is of the Muscovite type and unrelated to the period with which we are now concerned. The façades carry the usual frieze, below which they are entirely covered with flat reliefs (figure 61). The recesses of the frieze are occupied by figures of saints, and the space above is filled with complicated reliefs of scriptural scenes. Instead of the usual pilasters, there are at the corners heavy square columns with carved ornament, topped with decorative heads, sometimes on three sides. The pilasters which alternate with these columns are also covered with carvings. The pointed arch which as yet is hardly evident in the Church of the Nativity is expressed here both in the fronts of the vestibules and in the arches of the lateral frieze, where it is represented by an angular break in the external line. The niches between these columns of the frieze are occupied by sculptured high-relief figures standing on pedestals. Both the robed saints and the stalwart champions with spear and shield are gracefully executed and remind one of the relief of St George on the Vatopedi steatite plaque published by Schlumberger. The walls are filled with arabesques of Oriental style, formed of vines stringing from a single stem. The Oriental influence is also recognizable in the choice of the creatures depicted in relief. They include gryphons, sirens, centaurs, a wolf, and a whale, the latter resembling the bearded dragon of Western bestiaries. The method of depicting the whole animal kingdom headed by the elephant is pure Romanesque; the elephant is not saddled, but has a collar around his neck and his trunk hangs down. His ears are on the top of his head, instead of in the place where they ought to be, and his legs are hardly robust enough for a pachyderm, apart from the fact that they are equipped with long toes. The reliefs begin to show some decline in technique, particularly in the proportions of certain of the human figures.

The Romanesque elements are extremely numerous. The female masks on the corner impost blocks resemble closely those on the cathedral at Lund, in Sweden, erected in 1145. That church also shows the moustached masks of lion-like animals, the twining ornament, and many sorts of birds. The Romanesque style is also evident in a profile mask of a soldier with a helmet and a large ring in his ear. While so much of the ornament is out of place owing to stupid reconstruction, we find evidences of a frieze of lion-masks with a thick vine coming out of their mouths which resembles a similar frieze on St Martin's in Lyon (eleventh century), where the lion-masks are replaced by the human masks which appear in St George's over the loops of vine between the lions' heads. Masks with acanthus arabesques coming out of their mouths are fairly common in the West. The portals are of the simple Romanesque type. Where the earlier school used the same decoration around the doors as on the walls, St George's has a Virgin Intercessor, a St George, and two figures of Christ surrounded by arabesques.

Among the other Romanesque constructional forms introduced in the Vladimir-Suzdal area we find the quadrangular towers. The lower part of such a tower is preserved in Prince Andrew's favorite village of Bogolyubovo. Two stories are still standing (figures 62, 63). The lower shows a simple moulding and corbel table supported by almost disengaged columns and in the second story a triple window of Romanesque type. The corner pilasters have been attenuated into slender shafts with capitals, and the whole structure was, if Voronin's restoration is accurate, a remarkable example of the earlier Vladimir-Suzdal architecture (figure 62).

The monuments of this region and epoch represent the Russian variant of Western European Romanesque style expressed in white stone and combined with traditional Russo-Byzantine features. The fundamental difference between the Russian and Western European types lies in the Oriental motives in architecture and decoration. The ground plan of the church is fundamentally Byzantine, imported through Kiev, either a square with four columns or an oblong with narthex and six columns. The theme of the decoration, as we remarked a moment ago, is to be found in Psalm 148, and it is combined with decorative patterns of Oriental style covering the entire façades. The decorations of St George's in Yuryev Polski were added after the structure was completed, and show evidence of careful planning. The walls were divided into horizontal sections so that the more complex decoration above topped off a modestly adorned lower section. The round reliefs were executed separately and then inserted in the walls.

These Western reflexes reached the distant northeast partly through Galicia and Volhynia, as already noted, and partly through South Slavic masters from the Balkans who went to Russia to practice their craft, and the architectural developments which they stimulated came to an abrupt end with the invasion of the Tartars toward the middle of the thirteenth century. Russian mediaeval architecture certainly never produced anything more beautiful or harmonious than the Cathedral of the Assumption in Vladimir or the Church of the Virgin Intercessor at the Nerl River, and it is a tragedy of mediaeval culture that the catastrophe of the Tartar conquest interrupted the development of the national architecture at the very moment when its capacity to absorb new impulses was at its height.

*   *   *

After the Tartars had laid waste the southern and northeastern sections of Russia during the thirteenth century, all artistic interests lay dormant for a century and a half. Toward the close of the fourteenth century, as the Tartar power slowly disintegrated and the princes of Moscow began to create a nucleus around which the national spirit could once more rally, the impulse toward artistic creation showed signs of revival. The old architectural traditions lived on, though in greatly simplified forms. Sculpture was partially expressed in simple façade decoration. At the turn of the fifteenth century, when Western Europe was producing the great monuments of Renaissance art, fresh efforts were made in and about Moscow to construct large stone churches once more. The primitive art of the country as exemplified in wooden architecture still lived on, and formed the basis for what we may call the Muscovite Renaissance. The creative work of this new period consisted in gradually nationalizing the forms created in Vladimir-Suzdal, and partly also in Novgorod and Pskov, by the reaction of foreign influences.

The earliest Muscovite churches, insofar as they are preserved, show that the stone architecture of Moscow is a direct continuation of the architecture of Vladimir-Suzdal. The old church in the Kremlin, the little white stone chapel of the Redeemer in the Wood (*Spas na Boru*), which was built by Prince Ivan Kalita in 1330, (dismantled within the last few years and now destroyed), was a simple four-pillar church, and the pointed and profiled portals showed forms typical of the later school at Vladimir-Suzdal (figure 64). But by 1400 a new current is appreciable in Muscovite architecture which aims at the reproduction of the forms of Russian wooden architecture. It is time therefore to examine a few of the churches of the Muscovite transition style which are directly dependent on the models with which we are familiar from Vladimir-Suzdal.

The first such church is that of the Assumption of the Virgin at Zvenigorod, sixty kilometers west of Moscow, built in 1399, which in design still adheres to the Vladimir-Suzdal tradition (figure 65). It is built of white stone, cubical, and with a single cupola which rests on four arches borne by four heavy columns. The semicircular apses, three in number, are decorated with the profiles of slender columns. The pilasters at the corners that divide the façades have become the half-columns familiar from Vladimir-Suzdal, surmounted by lotus capitals. The complicated corbel-table decoration around the middle of the façades is here replaced by a carved stone frieze of triple pattern, which recurs at the top of the drum of the cupola and under the eaves of the apses. The pointed arches over the doorways and in the upper half of the façades between the pilasters correspond to models from Vladimir-Suzdal. The rather limited scale of form and decoration indicates native Russian workmanship.

The final stage of this transitional type from Vladimir-Suzdal to Moscow is represented by the Cathedral of the Annunciation in the Kremlin at Moscow itself, built between 1484 and 1489 by architects from Pskov (figure 66). Here we find the characteristic four-column plan from Vladimir-Suzdal combined with encorbelled arches. The wedge-topped barrel-like roof sections which add greatly to the decoration of the upper lines of the church are completely preserved. The apses are semicircular with the same diameter as the central cupola. The apses and cupola carry the traditional corbel-tables, but they resemble the type current at Pskov rather than at Vladimir.

The starting point for the new Muscovite art was the stone construction prevalent in the mediaeval northeast, but stone construction soon gave way to brick, and it is in the latter medium that the transition to the popular forms of wooden architecture was evolved. When the Muscovites began to build, at the end of the fifteenth century, they had no qualified native architects and so, like their Kievan forebears, they were obliged to call in foreign specialists. The latter were unfamiliar with the spirit and wealth of forms present in the native wooden architecture. Hence their churches are hardly national, and when able Russian builders developed they followed their own paths regardless of the precedents created by these casual foreigners.

Two churches in the Kremlin represent the work of foreign consultants. The first is the Cathedral of the Assumption, built by Ridolfo Fioravanti of Bologna in 1475-79 (figures 67 to 70). This church was first begun by Russian masters, but collapsed at the time of the earthquake of 1472. Fioravanti based his structure on the Assumption at Vladimir, but considerably simplified the design, since he copied only the older central part of the latter, though he retained the five cupolas (figure 68). He deepened the foundation to sixteen feet and connected the walls and arches by iron tie rods, beside lessening the stresses by constructing the arches of a special grade of light brick. The church itself is elsewhere built of white stone throughout and looks like an archaic example of Vladimir-Suzdal architecture. Its lines are severe and rather low, since Fioravanti used only Romanesque semicircular arches, and nowhere encorbelled or pointed ones. The façades have the conventional arched corbeltables resting on ornamental engaged colonettes, The actual work on this church was carried out by Russian artisans. Fioravanti instructed them in cement and brick manufacture and showed them how to use tie rods which facilitated widening the diameter of the arches. He also taught them the construction and use of mechanical hoisting appliances. All these new items of experience were also employed in the construction of the Cathedral of the Annunciation, which represents a considerably more advanced stage of architectural evolution in the Russian spirit than the Assumption, which antedates it by over five years.

As an example of foreign intervention in Russian architecture another neighboring church in the Kremlin, the Cathedral of the Archangel Michael (figure 71), built in 1509 by the Milanese architect Alevisio Novi, is of still greater interest. In ground plan and the use of five cupolas, the church presents almost a complete repetition of the Assumption in smaller dimensions. The façades are divided by an ornamental moulding, a row of semi circular vault-profiles appears at the top, though handled in Renaissance style. The façades resemble a two-storied Italian palazzo, although the interior is not so divided. The structure rests on a high stone base. The lower story has the form of arcades and the upper is divided into rectangular spaces crowned with scallop-shell niches. The asymmetry of the façade surfaces is due to shifting the internal columns toward the east, so that the cupolas appear off center. The façades recall fifteenth-century Venetian types. All decorative elements are of white stone, but the actual walls are red brick, a feature which is reminiscent of the Certosa in Pavia, and in general the church shows that its architect was familiar with North Italian architectural forms of the fifteenth century. The church built by Alevisio really stands further apart from the general movement of sixteenth-century Russian architecture than the Assumption designed by Fioravanti, but it contains motives which are picked up by the subsequent period of native Russian building.

After the liberation of Russia from the Tartar yoke, the newly awakened national consciousness sought other forms of ancient beauty preserved in wooden architecture, and with the aid of European technique it became possible to adapt these forms to the new brick style.

4. Moscow

4. Moscow

THE TARTAR invasion of 1238-1240 put an end to the rapid artistic evolution which had taken place in northeastern Russia during the previous seventy-five years. Toward the close of the fourteenth century, however, the impulse toward artistic creation once more showed signs of revival as the Tartar power disintegrated. With the rise of Moscow in the fifteenth century, we thus have a renaissance of Russian art exemplified by construction of new stone churches in and about Moscow as the nucleus of national recovery. At first, as we have seen, these churches largely reproduce the forms current in Novgorod, Pskov, and above all Vladimir and Suzdal, where Byzantine and Romanesque elements had been effectively combined. The starting point of the new Muscovite art was thus chiefly the stone construction prevalent in the northeastern churches of the twelfth century, which I described in the last chapter. But to these forms Moscow now adds a fresh element derived from the primitive national wooden architecture. It is with this wooden architecture and the reflexes of it in Muscovite stone and brick that we shall now concern ourselves.

We noted earlier that the earliest Christian churches in Russia, prior to the general conversion of the nation, were constructed of wood, and you remember that the first cathedral of Novgorod, which was built in 989 and after its destruction by fire in 1045 was replaced by the present stone cathedral of St Sophia, was also built of wood and had "thirteen roofs," ('vierkhi'), that is, pinnacles, gables, or cupolas. Though the wealthier cities subsequently vied with Kiev, Novgorod, and Vladimir in the erection of stone or brick edifices, the remote country districts which were either far from the quarries on the Volga or lacked the technique of brick manufacture were obliged to develop a style of their own for the construction of churches wholly made of wood. The tradition of skill in carpentry was most cultivated in the northern forested areas where pine and fir grow in profusion, and it is thus in the district north of the Volga, even well up under the Arctic circle, that the most interesting types of wooden architecture are preserved. These churches were built of undried logs and planks, and in consequence of the manifest impermanence of wood, could not be long-lived monuments. The earliest extant wooden churches thus go back no earlier than the end of the sixteenth century, and their erection ceased with the close of the eighteenth when urban brick architecture penetrated even the country districts. On the other hand, the innate conservatism of popular art, and the perfection of line and style evident in even the earliest extant wooden churches, quite apart from the mention of wooden churches of some complexity of design in early Russian mediaeval historical sources, prove that they exemplify the fruits of a long previous development and justify us in using these extant wooden churches as examples of what must have been the chief types of wooden architecture which exerted their influence on the Muscovite Renaissance of the sixteenth century. Many of the wooden churches which appear in the illustrations are thus younger than the Muscovite churches which were influenced by earlier and no longer existent wooden structures. It is thus as types, and not for their antiquity, that these wooden churches are primarily interesting.

The simplest and most primitive wooden churches differed in no respect from peasant huts, except perhaps that they had a cross on the roof. They were built either of unsquared or of rough-hewn logs either interlacing at the corners as in the American log cabin, or hewn down to wedge-shaped points which fitted snugly over and under each other. Such churches were built in oblong or octagonal shape. In the former case they had a two-sloped roof, in the latter an eight-sloped one corresponding to the sides of the structure itself. We should note that the logs of the building are laid horizontally, not vertically in stockade fashion as was the primitive custom in Scandinavia. The roof was built of planks, and the gaps between the logs were often stuffed with moss. As a matter of fact, the peasant carpenters of the north never used any tool except the axe even for smoothing out planks, and it is amazing what dexterity they acquired in performing difficult tasks with this single tool. Figure 72 shows a church constructed in Cherdynsk, in 1614, which is now almost reduced to kindling wood. It is built of roughly squared logs overlapping at the corners; the roof is made of planks, and the eaves are faced with planks. The church shows the characteristic sharp pitch of the roof which becomes even more marked in the further development of these structures. This church has a pentagonal apse, built apparently in imitation of the rounded apses of stone churches. It has a small cupola of onion shape, covered with oiled shingles made of aspen wood. While the apse shows traces of the influence of earlier brick or stone structures, no such influence is discernible in the better preserved church at Ust Padenga, 1675, of the same type which appears in figure 73. Here we have a projection for the apse as well as for the front vestibule, and the church presents the aspect of three sheds thrown together.

One pronounced characteristic of all Russian wooden architecture is a marked tendency to prolong the vertical lines. In churches of the simple oblong type, this tendency manifested itself in steep roofs, the gables of which were sometimes twice as high as the body of the church. The example shown, at Elgomski Pogost, 1643, (figure 74) has a vestibule in front, and the corresponding projection on the rear has become a somewhat reduced reproduction of the main body of the church. The next step in the development of this type of church was the addition of a basement, the purpose of which was to raise the church above the snow and, decoratively, to give it greater height among the humbler structures surrounding it (St John on the Ishna, near Rostov Veliki, 1687; figure 75). Here there occurs for the first time over the apse and vestibule an ornamental gable of onion section. While Russian scholars usually consider this type of gable an element of primitive wooden architecture, this point should not be too heavily stressed in view of the possibility that this onion-shaped section may be related to the pointed arch as it appears in Pskov and Novgorod, and thus represent an attempt to duplicate in wood either encorbelled vault ends with pointed arches of the type exemplified on the Cathedral of the Annunciation in the Kremlin, or even the semicircular vaults of the Vladimir churches. I referred also in the second chapter to the theory that these gables of onion-shaped section are the forerunner of the bulbous cupola, though personally I doubt the acceptability of any such view. This church also has the closed porch which is frequently repeated on more pretentious wooden structures and later becomes an element of Muscovite church architecture.

I mentioned a moment ago that some of the primitive churches were octagonal instead of oblong. At Chelmuzhe exists a church dating from 1605 in which the church itself is of the oblong type, built of squared logs, with a gabled apse surmounted by a very small open cylinder of onion section, while the cupola, which this time is tent-shaped, rests on an octagonal base (figure 76). This church provides a convenient transition to the second type of wooden structure, which we may call tower-churches. The distinguishing feature of this type is the fact that the tendency noticed in the oblong churches to prolong the vertical lines is further worked out by increasing the height of the primitive octagonal church, so that the main body of the church takes on the form of a tower. The eight slopes of the roof are then raised to a considerably higher level, forming a tent-shaped pyramidal spire. These spires are of varying heights and proportions, and are eventually adapted to the brick architecture of Moscow. Such tent-shaped spires are one of the few elements of Russian architecture which can rather definitely be traced to Oriental influence transmitted during the period of Tartar domination, and the discovery in the central Asian city of Chiva of a thirteenth-century mausoleum with a spire of this character seems to corroborate this opinion. The church of Panilovo, which dates from 1600, has the usual ornamental onion gable over the vestibule, which is reached by two flights of covered stairs and a porch (figures 77, 79, 80).

Uftiug (figure 78), is a striking type of octagon on cube construction, with tent-shaped spire, roofed porch and entrance stairway. This church, though built in the eighteenth century, is still constructed of unsquared logs. A variation of this type is supplied by Puchuga, 1698 (figure 81), where we have a pentagonal apse topped with an onion-section gable, and figure 82, Zachachie, represents a peculiarly fine example of an octangular church, with projecting apse, vestibule, and modified pyramidal cupola, constructed near Archangel in 1627. There are also types of wooden churches where the main body of the church is cubical, with a flat roof on which rest ornamental onion-section gables, intersecting with each other and serving as a base for the tent-shaped cupola. At Lampozhnya (figure 83) in the double apses of pentagonal shape we have a manifest effort to duplicate the multiple apses of stone architecture. This church dates from 1781.

The final type of wooden churches comprehends those of cross shape. In the example at Berezovets (figure 84) occurs an octagonal base expanded on four sides by arms all of which have rounded ends except the vestibule. The transepts, apse, and vestibule are surmounted by onion-section box gables, and on the roof of the main body of the church we find a cross-shaped penthouse supporting the cupolas. Notable here are the raised porches, an important feature later transmitted to Muscovite architecture. The further development of this type of church, by the addition of stepped gables, gives the opportunity for the use of multiple cupolas, as in the next example Vuitegorski Pogost (figure 85), which shows seventeen cupolas, and finally, the familiar church at Kizhi (figures 86, 87), which has twenty-two. We should note the narrow necks replacing the older drums as support of the cupolas, as this feature recurs in Muscovite architecture.

The development of the multi-cupolar church has a curious history. Among the people of the remoter districts after the Tartar conquest the round or octagonal church with tent-like spire was actually the traditionally favored silhouette, and toward the end of the fifteenth century the Russian annals mention one city where, after the old "round" (actually, octagonal) church had burned down, the inhabitants protested successfully against its being replaced by a new edifice of cruciform plan. At the time of the ecclesiastical reforms of the seventeenth century, which in general signalized a return to strictly Greek forms and observances, the further construction of round churches with pyramidal or tent-shaped spires was officially forbidden, and a return was prescribed to the Greek five-cupola type. It was this prescription which inspired the multi-cupolar churches, in which the cupolas take on a purely decorative function, and by their placement on recessive gables preserve the old popular pyramidal silhouette, as is the case at Kizhi.

While as time went on the wooden churches themselves were appreciably influenced, particularly as regards apses and cupolas, by the usages of masonry construction, it is also plain from the illustrations that basically these churches represent a path of artistic evolution quite distinct from the originally alien forms of stone and brick church architecture which prevailed in Russia prior to the Muscovite period. The history of wooden architecture in Eastern Europe is a subject of considerable importance, and has been recently brought to the fore by the researches and theories of Strzygowski, who traces the origins of Eastern European wooden architecture to the Ukraine. Further study will doubtless be rewarding.

The influences exerted by wooden architecture on the evolution of Muscovite construction stand out with some clarity from the previous description: (1) abandonment of the conventional four or six-column type of church with three apses and one or more cupolas; (2) increased emphasis on height as exemplified by the tower-churches with tent-shaped spire; (3) use for decorative purposes of the onion-shaped section as it appears on the gables or for their adornment; (4) introduction of entrance-porches and the use of external galleries for utility and decoration; (5) combination of the pyramidal spire with the cupola; (6) division of the church into two stories, the basement being surrounded by arcaded galleries, with a consequent decline in the decorative importance of the portals; and (7) the introduction of separate campanile towers, or belfries instead of the simple wall-belfry adjoining the church as we saw it developed at Pskov.

The first church in the neighborhood of Moscow which exemplifies an attempt at adapting the forms of wooden architecture to brick construction is that of St John the Baptist at Dyakovo, built about 1529 (figures 88, 89). This was a votive church erected by Basil III, the father of Ivan the Terrible, as an offering to assure the birth of a son to his second wife, Helena Glinskaya. It was dedicated to St John the Baptist because he too was the son of a father advanced in years; and since Ivan the Terrible was an offspring of Basil's second marriage, it would appear that his prayers were heard. This church signifies an abrupt break with the old tradition, but in a transitional sense. The architect obviously hesitated between cupola and pyramid, and arrived at a columnar

result. The church is devoid of internal columns. It consists
of an octagonal base surrounded by porches, but reflects the
cross-shaped wooden church by the placing of four independent octagonal chapels at the corners. It has one semicircular apse inclosed between the two corner chapels of the
east end, and an external vestibule at ground level on the west
façade. Its bells are suspended in a wall-belfry of Romanesque lines over the door of the latter. The actual silhouette
is that of the pyramidal spire. The central octagon carries a
low cupola of the old flat type supported on a polygonal base
by eight short thick half-columns. The base is joined to the
tower by two rows of decorative corbels, the upper pointed
and the lower semicircular, corresponding to the graduated
vaults within the church. The cupolas of the lateral chapels
are of the same type, but lack the columns under the cap,
which is sustained by three rows of angular corbels which are
simplified from the onion-section gables, or *kokoshniki*,
familiar from the more ornate wooden churches. The windows are all topped with angular pediments, while over the
portals we find semicircular arches. All plane surfaces are
decorated with rectangular frescoed panels. The use of
colored tiles for adornment exemplified here will appear
again in Moscow. Certain details of the decoration recall the
work of Alevisio Novi on St Michael's in the Kremlin. The
church is interesting, first, for its deviation from the old
conventions, and second, because it is the prototype of St
Basil's on the Red Square in Moscow.

A second church which moves still further toward an
approximation of the forms of wooden architecture is the
Church of the Ascension at the neighboring village of Kolomenskoye, also built of brick by Basil III in 1532 (figures

90, 91). Here we have a tower resting on a polygonal base decorated with arched corbel-table and pilasters, surmounting an octagonal body with which it is connected by three rows of *kokoshniki*, this time in the conventional shape. The angles are buttressed with heavy corners in the shape of square columns. The heavy superstructure rests on an extensive cross-shaped base in the form of galleries with a Romanesque arcade reached by three covered staircases. This church is one of the most graceful and beautiful of the whole Moscow area, and contemporaneous annalists praise it as unparalleled. Its affinity with wooden architecture is clearly apparent if you compare it with the cross-shaped church of the Assumption at Varzug in the province of Archangel, which also shows the use of *kokoshniki* as transitions from the gables on the arms of the cross to the pyramidal spire.

Another pyramidal church which shows rather more numerous reminiscences of the older architecture combined with new features derived from wood construction is that of the Transfiguration at Ostrov, a suburb of Moscow, erected about 1550 (figures 92, 93). The distinguishing feature of this church is the enormous number of the *kokoshniki;* in rounded form they support the drums of the cupolas over the chapels at the eastern corners, and in pointed form they provide a transition from the square base to the octagonal superstructure, and from the latter to a short pyramidal spire which here for the first time is surmounted by a drum and cupola. In the ground plan of this church, the square base is surrounded by a gallery wide enough to permit the erection at either side of the apse, which occupies the whole eastern dimension of the central square, of a separate chapel surmounted by a cupola and possessing an apse of its own. On the eastern façade the apses of the two chapels and the apse of the church itself combine to give the effect of the three apses of the pre-Muscovite churches. The carved decoration of apses and cupolas reminds us of churches in Pskov or the corresponding ornament on the cupolas of the Cathedral of the Annunciation in the Kremlin. The corner pillars of the rectangular main body are run into a corbel-table under the mouldings below the *kokoshniki* which form the transition to the pyramidal tower.

Probably the most striking monument of this period is the Church of Basil the Blest (figures 94 to 97), originally known as the Cathedral of the Virgin Intercessor, erected between 1554 and 1560 by Ivan the Terrible as a votive offering for the capture of Kazan from the Tartars. This church is so fantastic in design and execution that the foreign eye which rests upon it for the first time is in doubt whether to admire it as a consummate work of art or to despise it as a heap of junk. The best amateur comment I know of was made to me, as I was wandering around one day among its dark and forbidding chapels, by a young communist lady who asked, 'Don't you think this church typifies very well the mentality of Ivan the Terrible?' I believe she was right: the church has a neurasthenic aspect. It is set at the further end of the Red Square in Moscow, with the frowning wall of the Kremlin at the right and the mausoleum of Lenin below it, just visible beside the tower of the Historical Museum in the foreground (figure 94). Recalling the curious aspect of the church in Dyakovo, you can perhaps understand the elements of Basil the Blest. It was conceived by two Russian architects whose names are known: Posnik and Barma. The story that it was constructed by an Italian architect whom

Ivan caused to be blinded so he should not produce something more beautiful is completely apocryphal. Basically this is a cross-shaped church around a square center, over which rises the central cupola. Under the larger cupolas at each arm of the square are four other octagonal churches, and four others (two square and two of irregular outline) fill the spaces between the arms of the cross, being surmounted in their turn by four smaller cupolas. The belfry, consisting of a pyramidal spire set on a square, is separate from the church, at the southeast corner. St Basil's is thus a conglomeration of nine separate churches (figure 97). The central cupola is octagonal; then a series of ornate *kokoshniki* form a transition to a smaller octagon supporting the pyramidal spire, surmounted by a small bulbous cupola. The external gallery is most noticeable on the west front, where it is approached by covered staircases terminating in ornate porches which, like the landings, are topped with small pyramidal spires. It forms a sort of ambulatory inclosing the outside chapels. The church is constructed of white stone and red brick, and the polychrome effect is enhanced by the abundant use of colored tile. The eight cupolas are all different in design, as if to call attention to the various component chapels in the complex. Some are topped with ribbed designs either straight or spiral; others carry facets which make them look like pineapples; one is covered with tile resembling the aspen shingles of wooden churches, and another shows a honeycomb design. The panels of the four larger cupolas show a moulding rising to a sharp point which frames a small window. The cupolas all show the habitually bulbous Muscovite type projecting considerably beyond the diameter of the drum.

It requires a little examination and reflection before one

discovers the essential unity of this bizarre structure which probably represents the perfect apogee from the noble simplicity and silent grandeur of classic outline. Yet on the basis of the preceding elements of wooden architecture it is neither difficult of comprehension nor devoid of aesthetic appeal. The balancing of masses and the conical silhouette replace the rigorous symmetry of line which prevails even in most of the churches of the Vladimir-Suzdal school. It is perhaps worth noting that the modern Church of the Resurrection, erected in Leningrad on the site of the assassination of Alexander II, was inspired by St Basil's and reproduces its polychromy, particularly on the cupolas.

In view of the pyramidal character of the central element in St Basil's and its pyramidal silhouette as a whole, it belongs among the descendants of the so-called tower-churches of wooden construction. There are two other typical churches of this sort which deserve attention. The first is that of the Assumption (figure 98) in Uglich, a town on the upper Volga north of Moscow, chiefly famous as the scene of the tragic death in 1591 of Ivan the Terrible's ten-year old son Dmitri, whose childish ghost stalks behind the scenes of Mussorgski's opera 'Boris Godunov.' Built in 1628, this church is distinguished by three pyramidal spires standing in a transverse row across the church directly in front of the apses. They rest upon a box-like superstructure topped with *kokoshniki* above pilaster-strips. From this pedestal the spires rise without transitional ornament, except for a single row of *kokoshniki* around the base of the middle one. All are topped with small bulbous cupolas on slender necks. What is particularly interesting here is the reminiscence of Vladimir-Suzdal in the use of three apses decorated with the familiar arched corbel-tables and colonettes. While the apses thus reproduce the ornament of churches built in Moscow a hundred years before, the roofs of the apses are handled in a later style, being decorated with dwarfed spires resembling those of certain wooden churches referred to earlier in this chapter.

A more complicated example of the use of pyramidal spires, and one in which the spires have undergone considerable modification, is the church of the Nativity of the Virgin in Putinki (Moscow), built in 1652 (figure 99). This church is actually a composite structure made up of a church with three spires and, at right angles to it, with one spire, a chapel dedicated to the Burning Bush. The two structures are united at their intersection by a belfry. Here the towers are purely ornamental, being set loosely on the top of the vaults. The church was built almost contemporaneously with the Nikonian reforms which abolished the pyramidal spire, and this factor may explain the sudden reduction of the relative importance of the pyramidal element. What is interesting, at any rate, is the lengthening of the drum-like base under the pyramid, and, in the case of the cupola over the chapel, the replacement of the octagonal element by a round drum as if it had been originally intended to crown the latter with a conventional cupola. This church was of course built during the reign of Peter the Great's father, and in its stodgy ornateness typifies Muscovite decorative architecture within the fifty years prior to the eighteenth century, when contemporary Western forms won the day. The decoration of the roof of the chapel of the Burning Bush with a pyramidal series of recessed *kokoshniki*, as well as the frieze of *kokoshniki* over the moulding of the cornice, is particularly characteristic of this period, and repeats itself on most of the churches next to be noticed.

The gain in internal space resulting from the absence of columns in the wooden churches, together with the financial inability of some parishes to build large structures requiring columns to support the roof, and the restricted ground space sometimes available, resulted in seventeenth-century Moscow in a tendency to imitate wooden construction in the so-called columnless churches. The first example of this type, constructed of brick in 1593, is the little church of the Virgin of the Don (figure 100), which, if you disregard the semi-circular chapel at the corner, consists of a small cube-like body surmounted by one cupola on a slender neck on a pyramid of superimposed semicircular *kokoshniki*, with three small apses and two side vestibules. The exterior decoration is very simple, being composed only of mouldings and a cornice, with pointed *kokoshniki* over a moulding on the vestibules. A further evolution of this type is the Church of the Virgin Intercessor at Rubtsovo, near Moscow, built in 1626 (figure 101). This church consists of a small square with a gallery around three sides, three slightly projecting apses, and a chapel at either corner of the apse end. The whole structure is mounted on a basement, and the arches of the gallery were originally open. This church is one of the first constructed at Moscow after the so-called period of disorder following the death of Tsar Theodore, son of Ivan the Terrible, in 1598, since this epoch of unrest suspended all creative activity for a quarter of a century. With slight modifications this church also represents the basic structural model for most Muscovite churches of the seventeenth century, which also exerted a wide influence throughout the

whole area dependent upon Moscow. The chief modification
lies in increased height and in the resumption of the use of
five cupolas and emphasis on façade decoration, the latter
factor showing the reaction of baroque influence largely
imported from the Ukraine.

In the church of the Nativity of the Virgin in Putinki
(Figure 99), we noticed the very reserved use of pyramidal
spires, in line with the Metropolitan Nikon's prohibition of
this decorative element. In the Church of the Georgian
Virgin begun in 1628, but enlarged in 1653, we find the
change to the new official style fully developed (figure 102).
Here we have the same recessed *kokoshniki* covering the
vaults of the roof, but a considerably greater wealth of adornment on the cornices, while double columns replace the
simple pilasters. The cupolas rest on slender lantern-like
drums of smaller diameter, and the sole relic of a pyramidal
spire appears over the entrance porch. The same conventions
repeat themselves in the handling of two other Muscovite
churches of the seventeenth century, both dedicated to St
Nicholas. The first, known as St Nicholas in Stolpy (figure
103), is distinguished by its broad two-story gallery, above
which rises the mass of the church. Here the *kokoshniki* do
not present the extreme pointed type, but are almost semicircular, and only slightly recessed, while the roof of the
second church, St Nicholas in Pyzhi (figure 104), shows
the more recessed type rising in a pyramid on a smaller square
base. The next church, that of the Ascension in the
Potters' Quarter (*v Goncharakh*, figure 105), while showing a row of recessed *kokoshniki* at the cornice, uses them
only sparingly on the roof, and simply as ends for the vaulted
bases under the drums of the cupolas. The white trimmings

against the red-brick background give this church its distinctive character. In the church of the Trinity in Ostankino, near Moscow, built in 1668 (figure 106), they have a common base, supported on two rows of *kokoshniki*. This church exhibits the basic design of the columnless church. It rests on a high basement, and has two chapels at either corner of the eastern end, the apses of which unite with that of the main church to produce the antique three-apsed effect. The cupolas of the chapels also rest on two retreating rows of overlapping *kokoshniki*. The balustered cornices and the windows show the baroque style. The same predilection for florid style and exuberant ornament is shown in the Church of St Gregory (figure 107), erected in Moscow in 1679. This church was much admired by contemporaries. The cornice has a magnificent ceramic frieze. The belfry shows the time-honored plan of octagon on square, supporting a pyramidal spire, broken with baroque windows and topped by a small bulbous cupola.

Toward 1670, the rows of corbelled arches, which are most easily designated by their Russian name of *kokoshniki*, tend to disappear, and the drums of the cupolas begin to rise out of the corners of the roofs like so many stove pipes. This backward step was actually dictated by reasons of economy. Heretofore the roofs had been covered with lead sheets with soldered joints which were easily shaped to any given outline. About this time thin iron sheets joined with rivets began to replace lead, and this surface was difficult to handle over ornamental projections.

The last of the Moscow series, the Church of St Nicholas of the Great Cross, named for a relic deposited in it, dates from the close of the seventeenth century, and represents the height of baroque infiltration in Moscow itself. The church has been dismantled. It had the conventional five cupolas on slender drums of the characteristic seventeenth-century type. The cupolas were embossed with raised six-pointed stars, and the drums decorated with slender colonettes turned in spirals. The scallop-shell niches were copied from St Michael's, and this motive is repeated under the drums of the cupolas. The superposed pilasters and the division of the façades also remind us of the former church, with its Italian manner (figures 71, 108).

We have now arrived at a period where foreign artists were being extensively employed in Moscow, and apart from the five cupolas St Nicholas' has scarcely any Russian elements at all. The pyramidal tradition returns once more, however, in the suburban church of the Virgin Intercessor at Fili (figure 109), built in 1693 by the maternal uncle of Peter the Great. Here the decorative effect is secured with a minimum of ornamentation. Like the church at Kolomenskoye, this church is raised on a terrace reached by three heavy staircases. The edifice is in the form of a cross with the ends of the arms rounded. Over this base rises a series of octagonal prisms culminating in a small cupola. The windows are crowned with cock's-comb pediments. The church possesses extraordinary beauty and grace, which is more than can be said for most of the contemporary monuments of Moscow itself. We should perhaps end our series with this intriguing structure, but it is worth while to compare it with an architectural monstrosity (if you will pardon the term) perpetrated in the same decade. This is the Church of the Miraculous Virgin at Dubrovitsy, near Moscow (figure 110). The church was built by Vasili Galitsin, the lover and confederate of Peter the Great's half-sister Sophia, who acted as regent during Peter's minority and did her best to prevent his reaching the throne. This is a white stone structure on a quatrefoil base. The tower, which looks like an ivory rattle, is completely covered with poorly executed decorative sculpture. If St Basil's reflects the mentality of Ivan the Terrible, this church certainly is a stone symbol of that of Galitsin, a Muscovite devoted to an unassimilated Western culture. The church thus typifies the state of mind of many progressive Russians at the moment when Peter the Great came to the throne, and therefore possesses a sentimental importance out of all proportion to its trifling artistic merit.

Before closing, I should like to contrast this un-Russian product with an almost contemporary manifestation of pure Russian art under Muscovite influence at Yaroslavl, on the Volga. The Church of St John (the Baptist), built in 1687, is one of the finest examples of Russian polychrome decoration (figures 111 to 113). Here the architects were not cramped for space or funds, and could exceed the modest dimensions of the Muscovite columnless churches, though their basic design follows this type. St John's thus has fifteen cupolas, all gilded, which contrast brilliantly with the soft red of its walls, in which are set lines of blue tiling. Most of the cupolas rise directly from the roof without any ornamental base. The church is a rectangle of the four-column type with three apses, surrounded on three sides with a gallery terminating at the apse and with two chapels rounded into apses of equal size with those of the church. The walls of the apses are facetted like the Granitovaya Palata in the Kremlin. This church is the last great monument of Russian architecture of the Muscovite school, and in its composition lacks the baroque elements which typify the transition from Muscovite to the absorption of Russia into the currents of international art which flow in the eighteenth century.

We have now completed our rather rapid tour of Russian churches from the Byzantine types of the eleventh century to the infusion of Ukrainian baroque after 1650. We noted the standard Kievan type of the six-column basilica with three apses, later copied at both Novgorod and Vladimir-Suzdal, and modified into the four-column church with single cupola. I emphasized that the two great cathedrals of St Sophia more or less stand alone in their districts as monuments of individual style. We saw the solidity and simplicity of Novgorod construction, and the influences of two successive schools of Byzantine painting on decoration of the northern churches. We remarked the introduction of some Western influences in the development of the four-gable roof and in façade decoration at Novgorod and Pskov. Yet the most striking adaptation of Romanesque elements to a Byzantine base occurred in the great churches at Vladimir, which stand out as the most distinguished examples of mediaeval Russian architecture before the Tartar conquest. We found that the Tartar invasion and rule marked a serious break in the Russian architectural tradition, but, as it weakened the adherence to the Byzantine norm, it also stimulated the injection of elements of primitive wooden architecture into the stone and brick structures of the Muscovite Renaissance. Here the Byzantine influence becomes a distant memory, except in learned and deliberate imitations, and as Peter the Great flings wide the doors to Western culture, Russia abandons its mediaeval traditions to follow the contemporary schools of the West.

Index

Index

Illustrations

1. Kiev—Desyatinnaya church

2. Kiev—St Sophia

3. Kiev—St Sophia

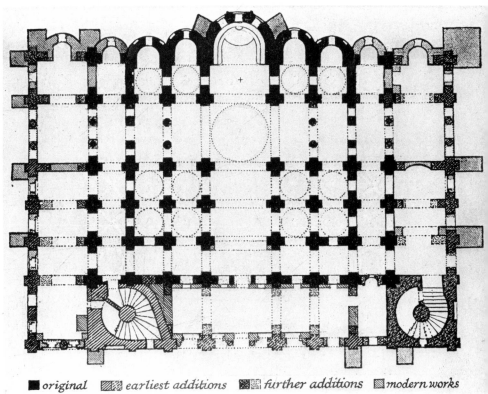

■ *original* ▨ *earliest additions* ▩ *further additions* ▨ *modern works*

4. Kiev—St Sophia

5. Kiev—St Sophia

6. Kiev—St Sophia

7. Kiev—St Sophia

8. St Sophia, Hippodrome scene

9. Chernigov—Cathedral of the Transfiguration

10. Chernigov—Yeletsa Monastery

11. Kiev—Church of the Assumption,
Crypt Monastery

12. Kiev—Church of the Assumption, Crypt Monastery

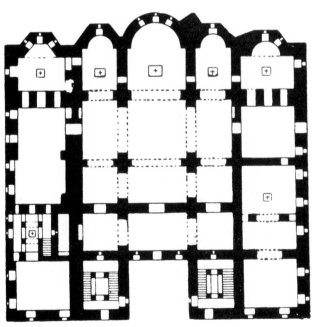

13. Kiev—Church of the Assumption, Crypt Monastery

14. Kiev—Monastery of St Michael

15. Kiev—Monastery of St Michael (mosaic)

16. Kiev—St Cyril (fresco)   17. Kiev—St Cyril (fresco)

18. Novgorod—St Sophia

19. Novgorod—St Sophia, restoration

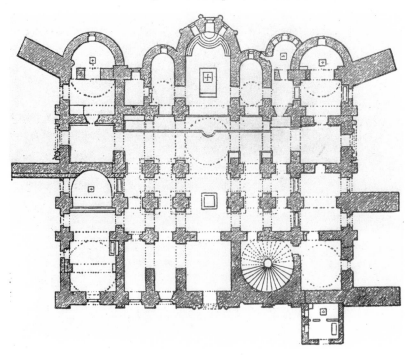

20. Novgorod—St Sophia, later state

21. Novgorod—St Sophia

22. Novgorod—St Sophia

23. Novgorod—St Sophia

24. Novgorod—St Nicholas the
Wonder-worker

25. Novgorod—St George

26, 27. Novgorod (Nereditsa)—Church of the Saviour
Before restoration   After restoration

28. Novgorod (Nereditsa)—Virgin (fresco)

29. Novgorod (Nereditsa)—Christ as Priest
(fresco)

30. Novgorod (Nereditsa)—Baptism (fresco)

31. Lipno—St Nicholas

32. Kovalyovo—Church of the Redeemer

33. Volotovo—An Angel (fresco)   34. Volotovo—Joseph (fresco)

35. Volotovo—Nativity (fresco)

36. Novgorod–St Theodore Stratilates

37. Novgorod—Church of the Transfiguration

38. Pskov—Church of the Transfiguration

39. Pskov—Church of St John the Baptist

40. Pskov—St Sergius

41. Pskov—St Basil

42. Dubrilov Gospel, 1164—Onion don

43. Kideksha—SS. Boris and Gleb

44. Pereyaslavl Zalesski—Church of the Transfiguration

45. Vladimir—Cathedral of the Assumption

46. Vladimir—Cathedral of the Assumption

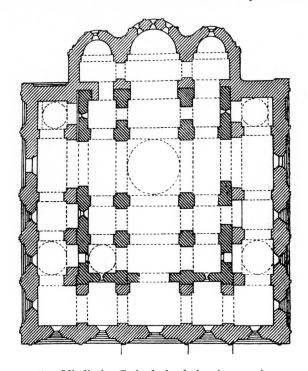

47. Vladimir—Cathedral of the Assumption

48. Vladimir—Cathedral of the Assumption

49. Vladimir—Cathedral of the Assumption

50, 51. Vladimir (Bogolyubovo)—Church on the Nerl River

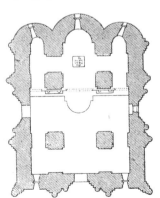

52. Vladimir (Bogolyubovo)—Church
on the Nerl River

53. David relief

54. Gryphon relief

55. Vladimir—St Dmitri

56. Vladimir—St Dmitri (fresco)

57. St Dmitri (fresco)

58. Suzdal–Cathedral of the Nativity of the Virgin

59. Suzdal–Basket capitals

60. Yuryev Polski—St George

61. Yuryev Polski—Detail of Carvings

62. Vladimir (Bogolyubovo) — Cathedral restoration

63. Extant tower

64. Moscow (Kremlin)—Church of the Redeemer in the Wood

65. Zvenigorod—Church of the Assumption

66. Moscow (Kremlin)—Cathedral of the Annunciation

67. Moscow (Kremlin)—Cathedral of the Assumption

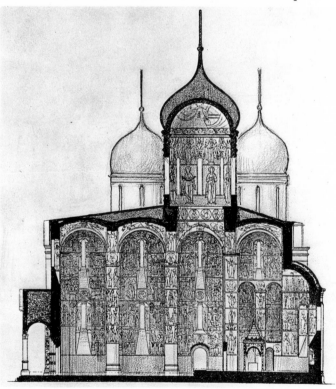

68. Section

69. Moscow (Kremlin)—Cathedral of the Assumption, looking east

70. Looking west (Coronation of Alexander II)

71. Moscow (Kremlin)—Cathedral of St Michael

72. Cherdynsk—Wooden church

73. Ust Padenga—Wooden church

4. Elgomski Pogost—Monastery church

75. Rostov Veliki—St John on Ishna River

76. Chelmuzhe—Wooden church

77. Panilovo—Wooden church

78. Uftiug—Wooden church

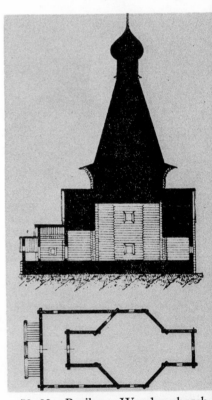

79, 80. Panilovo—Wooden church

81. Puchuga—Wooden church

82. Zachachie—Wooden church

83. Lampozhnya—Wooden church

84. Berezovets—Wooden church

85. Vuitegorski Pogost—Wooden church   86. Kizhi—Wooden church

87. Kizhi—Wooden churches and belfry

88, 89. Dyakovo—Church of St John the Baptist

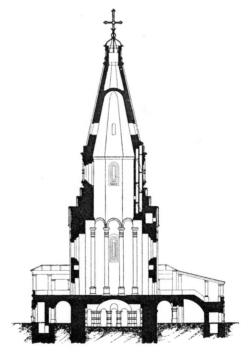

90, 91. Kolomenskoye—Church of the Ascension

92, 93. Ostrov—Church of the Transfiguration

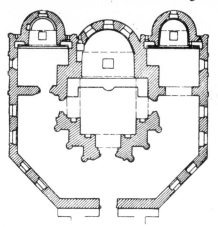

94.   Moscow—Red Square, Church of Basil the Blest

95, 96, 97.   Moscow—Church of Basil the Blest

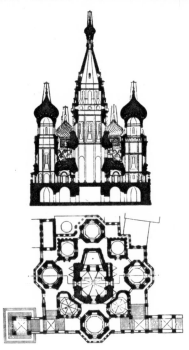

98. Uglich—Church of the Assumption

99. Moscow (Putinki)—Church of the Nativity of the Virgin

100. Moscow—Church of the Virgin
of the Don

101. Moscow (Rubtsovo)—Church of
the Virgin Intercessor

102. Moscow—Church of the
Georgian Virgin

103. Moscow (Stolpy)—St Nicholas

104. Moscow (Pyzhi)—St Nicholas
Detail showing *kokoshniki* and domes

105. Moscow—Church of the
Ascension in the Potters' Quarter

106. Moscow (Ostankino)—Trinity church

107. Moscow—St Gregory

108. Moscow–St Nicholas of the
Great Cross

109. Moscow (Fili)–Church of the
Virgin Intercessor

110. Moscow (Dubrovitsy)–Church of
the Miraculous Virgin

111. Yaroslavl–St John the Baptist
Detail

112. Yaroslavl—St John the Baptist, west view

113. Yaroslavl—St John the Baptist, east view